BELOVED

*A wife's journey with grief,
experiencing mercy and grace*

JULIE WILLERSDORF

D.O.L.L.

Daughters of Love & Light
www.daughtersofloveandlight.com
Adelaide, South Australia
admin@daughtersofloveandlight.com

© Julie Willersdorf 2021

ISBN: 9780645095173

All rights reserved. Except for private study, research, criticism or reviews, as permitted under the Copyright Act, no part of this book may be reproduced, stored in a retrieval system, or transmitted in any form or by any means without prior written permission. Enquiries should be made to the publisher.

Publisher's Note: This is a work of non-fiction. Names of persons have been used with permission.

Scripture quotations from The Authorized (King James) Version. Rights in the Authorized Version in the United Kingdom are vested in the Crown. Reproduced by permission of the Crown's patentee, Cambridge University Press.

Hymns *How Great Thou Art* and *I Surrender All* are in the public domain.

Cataloguing-in-Publications entry is available from the National Library of Australia http:/catalogue.nla.gov.au

First edition published 2021

*A book not just for those who are grieving
but for those who dare to go deeper in the Lord.*

Dedication

I dedicate this book firstly to my Lord, Jesus Christ.
There would be no book without Him.
He prompted me to begin this task and helped me produce
the first draft in less than a month.

I also dedicate this book to my late husband, Ian Willersdorf,
to our children and grandchildren, to my now deceased mum,
Valda McDonald and Ian's mum, Valerie Willersdorf.
Both our mums lost their husbands at age 55, but Ian's mum
has not only been widowed once but twice, both husbands
passing suddenly.

She has had to face the same with her eldest son, Ian.

Introduction

A Tale that is Told

'... we spend our years as a tale that is told.'
Psalm 90:9b

On December 9th, 2013 Ian Willersdorf, age 54, fell and collapsed while working with sheep, and despite his 30–year–old son's attempts to revive him, he passed from this life into glory. His sudden death is a shock to all his family and friends. Through this challenging time in her life, Ian's wife, Julie, finds all her needs, emotional, physical, and spiritual met through her Lord and Saviour, Jesus Christ.

This book is an excerpt of God's work in the life of an ordinary person, willing to take God at His Word – A tale being told in the hope of encouraging others to trust God with that simple child–like faith, taking Him at His Word. What other amazing stories would then be told!

'Our lives are like plotlines in a novel, with God as the author. In literary terms, I have heard it said that there is no such thing as a Christian tragedy because, though tragic things may happen to the Protagonist, the Christian always ends up in the arms of God. Death is not the last word. Disaster only brings the Christian closer to God...

Because of the cross, we may march through earthly jungles, deserts, gardens, cities, but we are on a heavenly trek. No matter what our journeys lead us through, we always end up in God.' – Leslie Williams

This quote by Leslie Williams sums up the writing of this book. May you be blessed as you follow the heavenly trek through the words which tell this part of Julie's story.

Chapter 1

The Phone Call

One phone call can change a life forever!
It was December 8th, 2013. Ian, myself, and eight of our eleven children were saying our goodbyes to Ian's mum. We had been to our annual home–school conference in Melbourne and then onto Kaniva to visit with his mum. Each year the children play their instruments in a concert with their grandma for the Senior Citizens Christmas Party.

As we were saying our goodbyes, one of the children made a suggestion. 'Mum why don't you and Dad travel home together in the crewman, just the two of you. Paul can drive the F250 and I can drive the Honda.'

We had travelled in three separate vehicles as Ian and the guys had been working away in two different places during the week previous.

One of the younger sons chimed in, 'Yeah Mum, Dad, then you can be together on the way home.'

Ian and I looked at each other and smiled. No one had to twist our arms. Ian had been away all week and to travel the eight to nine hours together without children was a real treat. However, none of us knew just then how special that would be.

As we travelled we were able to chat freely without the interruption of one child or another, one saying they were hungry or one wanting the music louder. After going through Deniliquin we were now passing the large sheep property where Ian had worked some 15–20 years earlier. He was employed as their accountant and company secretary, not that he was a qualified accountant. I looked past the paddock to the line of trees, trying to locate the tallest one. Yes, there it was. Just behind that tree was the house we had lived in.

I pointed in that direction, 'I wonder if there's anyone living there?' Ian shrugged. 'Don't know. It'd be nice to see what it's like now though.'

'I wonder if we could do that sometime. Would Robyn still be working in the office?'

'Not sure, but apparently she was, last I heard, which was a year or two ago.' I was drawn back in time as memories of our life in this place we were now just passing through, played one by one before me. Perhaps Ian too was reminiscing.

Ian was listening to the cricket, so I decided to catch up on my reading of Psalms. The first verse in chapter 34 particularly caught my attention: 'I will bless the Lord at all times: His praise shall continually be in my mouth.' I stopped reading and gazed out the window, but my focus was on nothing organic.

Bless the Lord at all times? ... at all times? No matter what? Praise Him continually? What a tall order, what a challenge! However, deep within my heart came, *That is what I want to do. That is who I want to be.*

Quietly I prayed, 'Lord I want this verse to be real to me, I want these words to be mine – that I would bless You at all times and my mouth would continually praise You.'

Then, came the next afternoon ...

'Hello, Julie Willersdorf speaking.' It was my usual response to answering the phone.

However, I wasn't prepared for my son's reply. His voice, strained and urgent coming through the phone, vibrated through my ear, and into my whole being. I knew something was wrong. 'Something's happened to Dad. You . . . you better pray.'

My mind was racing. I breathed deep, then replied, 'What's happened?'

'He . . . He's just collapsed. The ambulance is here, but I'm not sure how he is.'

The phone call ended. An emotional rollercoaster started. My stomach felt like cream churning into butter. *I wish I knew exactly what happened. What am I meant to do?* Part of me wanted to go where they were. I also knew I needed to be here with my other children.

I gathered the four children around, took a long breath and said, 'Something's happened to Dad; I'm not sure how he is. It sounds bad, but remember, God does all things well, and we can trust Him no matter what.'

Where had those words come from? While staying with my mother–in–law, we watched a DVD of the testimony of a man's mother who had polio and spent two years in an iron lung. The rest of her life she was strapped into a wheelchair. It was an amazing testimony of tragedy and triumph through suffering. The Lord used her powerfully in His service, from that wheelchair. She was able to be victorious in such terrible adversity because she learnt to live in the secret place of the Most High.

Her son shared three things which she learnt and lived: God does all things well, God is all–powerful, and be thankful in all things. Little did I know the importance of watching that DVD that night.

Now, in spite of my uncertainty and anxiousness, the Lord brought those words from the DVD back to me to help us in that moment.

'Let's pray! Father God, we don't know what has happened to Dad, but you do. We pray You will be with him and David and the ambulance officers. Help us to trust You. We ask this in Jesus' name.'

I was trying to think clearly as to what to do next, but my mind was once again on a racing track: *What has happened? How bad is he? Will I need to go to the hospital? When should I go? No, I can't go until I hear more.* I tried to put the questions aside and busied myself preparing the evening meal early, just in case.

About half an hour later the phone rang again. I quickly picked it up, hungry but hesitant for the news it would bring me. Yes, it was David's voice but what was he saying? I could barely make out his words they were so, so . . .

'Jesus, Jesus' was all I could hear. *Was he crying?*

'What are you trying to say David?' Fear was creeping over me. 'What are you trying to say?' I paused breathing, intently listening, waiting, straining to hear.

Through a strained voice shrouded by sobs and tears he replied, 'Dad's gone! Gone to be with Jesus!'

I was numb, standing as if turning to stone. Shock I guess, seeping, slowly throughout my body, a stepping from reality into a dream, no, a nightmare. The churning of cream had now produced a lump of butter in my stomach, but unlike soft butter, it sat like a hard rock. I felt ill.

That call heralded in the total change of my life from married woman to widow and single parent. And that Monday afternoon I became a widow at 53.

Does God put us to the test and take us at our word? *What did I ask only just yesterday: to praise God continually and to make it real? But now, in this situation – to bless the Lord?*

Chapter 2

Is It True?

Two of my children waited expectantly as I hung up the phone. They had heard my side of the conversation, and no doubt saw my reaction of total shock. They knew things weren't good, but they didn't know how bad.

How does one tell your children their dad has just died? How does one even process that themselves? That your life partner, your other half, the one you share everything with – the good, the bad, the fun, the struggles, the babies who grow and marry to produce grandbabies – is no longer there. There was no escaping what I had to do.

'That was David.' My throat was tight as if someone was grabbing it and not letting go. I could feel that hard lump of butter now a stone in my stomach sitting heavy in the bottom but now rolling about as if tossed by waves. Part of me tried to maintain control – that part that was still in disbelief. My mind grappled with the news, still trying to process it and yet having to inform someone else as if it were true. *I don't want it to be true!*

Dad's gone...' The choking in my neck was making it hard. 'Gone . . . to be with Jesus.' I had said it! As much as I protested, it must be true. Now the floodgates opened, theirs and mine. The news had been an unexpected blow that breaks the skin, a raw, open wound. We each felt the pain and wanted it fixed: to make the bleeding stop and all made better. But it would never be the same again – there would remain a deep scar always. We sought, and we comforted, as we hugged and cried together.

My two youngest children were playing on the back lawn. I needed to tell them. *Oh God, this only gets harder.*

How do I tell my nine-year-old son, Jaden, his dad is no more, that he will never see him again; never sneak around the table after dinner to climb on his knee and play the 'beautiful dessert' game as they try to lick each other's ears?

How do I tell my six-year-old boy that he will never be able to play tackles with his dad ever again, never be able to play the 'trouble' chair game with him?

As my daughter and I walked out the back door to where the two were playing, they looked up. Their faces looked puzzled and expectant as they saw our reddened eyes. Somehow, I told them what David had said, but they still looked puzzled. I tried to explain further.

'Dad, Dad has just . . . died.' It sounded so blunt and so final!

They hung their heads, but no tears came. Their dad had always been their dad. Wasn't he always going to be here? How could he not be still alive?

We all felt the unreality of it because we all saw him in the morning and surely, surely, he would be coming home from work later. As with 'Doubting Thomas' we were silently saying, 'unless you can prove it to me, I can't believe it.' Or is it, 'I don't want to believe it. It can't be true.'

If only!

Chapter 3

God Does All Things Well

Michaela, my other daughter, had woken that morning unwell, her head throbbing, aching all over, and running a high temperature and so had been sleeping most of the day. She hadn't known anything about the two phone calls. *She does not need this just now, but I know I have to tell her. Oh God, how do I do this? I have never been here before apart from my father's death when I was twenty–two. We were all there as he took his last breath, and it was my older siblings who took charge of things.*

I went to her room to see if she was asleep or awake. 'Michaela are you awake?' She moaned and turned to look at me through half opened eyes. 'I need to tell you something.' I waited for her to rouse further. I took a deep breath. My already wet eyes began to fill again. 'Michaela, I've got some really bad news.' She still looked sleepy but waited for me to continue. 'Dad's gone! He's gone to be with the Jesus.' Those words were abhorrent to me. My heart, my mind, my whole being, protested: *Can this be true? I don't want it to be true!*

As I looked at her, she seemed still half asleep and dreaming. 'Thank you, Lord,' was her initial response. 'I don't know what you're doing but thank you anyway.' Michaela shared with me sometime later that she had had a dream about her dad dying which had disturbed her, but she felt the Lord asking her to trust Him. Now as she stood up her emotions caught up with the realisation of what I had told her. I saw her face change, like a shadow of a dark cloud slowly obscuring the sunlight. The tears came, no, sobs, as we hugged. Bethany joined us, and Ian's three girls, arms entwined, grieved as one, for their husband and father.

The realisation came that I had other children who needed to know. Ian's mum too. And my sister and brothers. I needed to tell them.

I picked up the phone to ring. After a pause, I took some deep breaths, trying to compose myself for what I had to say. I began, 'I've got some really bad news.' I could hardly breathe for the lump now in my throat. I held my upper chest. My eyes moistened. I tried to steady my voice, but it came out jerkily. I can't remember what exactly I said to each one as it all melted into a blur. Most thought the bad news I was bringing was the death of my elderly mother. If only that were the news!

As I made the calls, I was on automatic pilot, doing the next thing while internally my stomach was seasick. At times during the phone calls, a pause in the conversation would come as the realisation took hold both ends of the handpiece. I would tap my chest, trying to get breath while choking on the words as they tried to come out.

My daughter in law, Beck arrived. More tears, more hugs. Over the afternoon and evening more sons, my other two daughters in law and grandchildren arrived. As each one appeared the emotions, I had settled nicely while in my autopilot mode, would erupt and spill over. Together we shared our grief and sorrow. My husband was gone, but my family were all here. We were united, all experiencing the same loss. Somehow, I had let them all know, and they had come to gather around me and I around them. That was God's grace, His amazing Grace helping me.

Not only did God take me at my word that day traveling home with Ian, but He also provided the grace I needed. I had asked, 'Lord I want this verse to be real.' Later, one of my sons told me about the time I rang him with the news of his father's passing. He said, 'Mum, I will always remember what you told me that day.'

'What was that? I can't exactly remember.' I was curious.

'After you told me about Dad you said, 'Remember, God does all things well'.'

No, I hadn't remembered but that day and over the next twelve months God has stilled my soul and is still making all things well.

Chapter 4

A Father's Legacy

We received the gut-wrenching news concerning Ian about 2 pm that day, and later that afternoon I saw my eleven-year-old son, Rohnen, sitting at the table writing something. Tears welled up in my eyes when later he presented me with an order of service for his father's funeral. I selected portions of it and included it below:

Dad, the best dad for me!
Ian Paul Willersdorf 16 Feb 1959 – 9 Dec 2013
54 years

Lord, why did you take my Dad?
I'm ever so sad!
You take my Dad,
So You made me sad.
Yet, I still will praise your name,

BELOVED

Also, I will rejoice and thank you, now in the presence of all your people. Dad, you're called back home to be with Jesus, where you, me and all the ones that follow Jesus will live forever with Him, the Prince of Peace, Wonderful Counsellor, the Risen One, the Messiah. Lord thank you for giving my Dad 54 years to live, quite a long time. Oh! I so wish he could see his children's children, for this is his favourite verse in the Bible: '... for he will see his children's children and peace upon Israel' Psalm 128:6. God's plans are always best.

Your loving son,
Rohnen Jonathon Willersdorf

Thank you for coming all of you. While you honour Dad, you also honour Mum, Luke, David, Joel, Michaela, Paul, Raphael, Benjamin, Bethany, Rohnen, Jaden, and Shiloh.

Some months after this I came across a letter Rohnen had written to Ian and me earlier in the year. I had forgotten all about it but remembered showing it to Ian at the time. As I re-read the letter, my eyes welled with tears again.

To dear Mum, I like you for everything. Smacks are not pleasant, but I will praise the Lord for all 'bad and good' in mine and God's eyes. But most of all you love me. Thank you very much.

To dear Dad, thank you for letting me go to work with you. Thank you for all you have done. Dad, I pray that you and Mum will become and be some of the GREATEST in the Kingdom of God.

JULIE WILLERSDORF

To Dad & Mum, I hope that JESUS will come before you die or you will see your great, great grandchildren. If you die, it will be then close to my death, for great will be the mourning from my lips.

Thank you very much. Lots and lots and lots and lots and lots of love,
From your loving son Rohnen J. Willersdorf
Dad xxxxxxxxx ooooooooo Mum xxxxxxxxx ooooooooo
Both oooooo xxxxxx

Chapter 5

He Giveth His Beloved Sleep

At the closing of that fateful day, I was alone to face the night.

What a day it has been! I feel frozen even though it is hot. My eyes feel like I've been awake too long, red and bloodshot. My head is heavy, not exactly aching, more like a pressure valve wanting release. I am exhausted as I make my way to bed, going through the motions of the normal routine before climbing in.

As I lie here, the scenes of the day play back in my mind. It still feels unreal, a dream, a nightmare, but as I reach out my hand he's not there. If only it were a dream but where once Ian would lie is empty, and I cannot ignore the stark reality of it. I used to lay my head on his chest, his arm around me. I would hear his heartbeat, and before dropping off to sleep, he would speak a blessing over me and I over him. But tonight, there is silence.

It's true, but I don't want it to be. I cannot deny the fact. Ian's gone! I hug his pillow. I place it where he would have lain and put my head on it. The pressure valve opens a little. The pillow absorbs my tears.

'Father God help me! How do I do this? How do I go on without Ian?' I continue hugging and stroking the pillow, but it's not firm enough, not real enough, not alive. It's not Ian. I toss and turn, unable to settle as the stark truth dances loudly before me. I turn my head and look out the window into the night sky. The stars shimmering catch my eyes. They seem to beckon me to look higher. A song comes to mind. I start to sing it:

'Oh Lord my God! When I in awesome wonder
Consider all the works Thy hands have made.
I see the stars; I hear the roaring thunder,
Thy power throughout the universe displayed.'

My thoughts rise with the words of the song, 'How Great Thou Art.' They take me far above my grief and sadness to the one who is all powerful yet who is love and who brings comfort. The pressure is released. A sense of peace comes over me; I close my eyes and only wake with the morning light.
'He giveth His beloved sleep.' – Psalm 127:2b

Chapter 6

The Goodness of God, the Kindness of People

The phone rang hot over the next few days. I tried to compose myself between calls, convince myself I was OK, but the phone rings and makes me a liar. *I'm OK. I can do this. I'm fine; I'm fine.* I find out who it is. I hold my breath, my throat tightens. I try to speak. I was holding back the dam wall nicely but now the ring of the phone, the person now talking has caused cracks to appear in the wall and as I try to speak the cracks turn into gaping fissures, and I cannot mend them all. The damned–up water spills through and I'm a mess, and so are they. We cry together.

My son, David is behind me, but I only know because he is rubbing my shoulders. Every time the phone rings he is there. A giant of a man at six feet four inches tall but that gentle, caring touch – that is what makes him a giant of a man.

One of those phone calls was the mother–in–law of my son, Joel, telling me she has set up a donation site for people to donate money to me. She wanted to link it to a PayPal account and wanted to know if I had one. Again, my voice evaded me.

The kindness and goodness of people undo me. I become so overwhelmed, the tears well up, breathing becomes hard, and speech is lost.

Over the coming weeks as I checked that account I would yet again unravel, yet again be brought to tears, yet again be lost for words as I see so many people donating money and offering words of comfort. Some are even strangers who have never met me. 'We are friends of friends but know what it is like to have a father die early. May the Lord bless you and keep you, shine His face down upon you and give you peace.'

'We don't know Ian and his family but have heard the sad news though some friends. Our sympathy is with you all, as are our prayers. God knows you need this money ($1,000) more than we do.'

A knock at the door brings two ladies from church, laden with pies and cakes. I come unzipped. I thought I had contained all those emotions, but no zip is too tight for grief. His fingers are ever ready – a phone call, a visitor, a memory; goodness and loving–kindness shower me and I'm all undone.

It reminds me of what the Bible says in Isaiah 63:7. 'I will mention the loving kindnesses of the Lord, and the praises of the Lord, according to all that the Lord hath bestowed on us, and the great goodness toward the house of Israel, which he hath bestowed on them according to his mercies, and according to the multitude of his loving kindnesses' and Rom 2:4b says, 'the goodness of God leadeth thee to repentance.'

Through the phone calls, the cards, the money, the food, came God's loving kindness with skin and flesh and blood on. The goodness of God led me to humbleness, to tearfulness, to gratefulness. Yes, I was undone! But I needed to be. Release had to come so that thankfulness and gratefulness could flow.

Chapter 7

I Come to the Garden Alone

Early this morning at 5:30 I chose to walk in my garden. A song came to mind, so I sang, 'I come to the garden alone...' an old song, a favourite since a little girl. I was thinking about the words of the song as I sang them: about walking and talking with Jesus; about the joy we share together in the garden. What beautiful words! I began the song again, 'I come to the garden alone...' I faltered on that last word.

I saw a white garden chair and sat down. Alone: how the meaning, the feeling, the knowing of that word filled my being as my thoughts again turned to my most dear, beloved, husband, who, suddenly and without warning went to be with the Lord less than a week ago.

Alone! I feel so lonely, so abandoned!

Alone! Yet, I have children, grandchildren, friends about me.

Alone! Two who were one, ripped apart and half left, on their own.

I protested: *I don't want to be alone!*

But who was the song talking about? Who have I come to meet in the garden this morning?

In the depths of my aloneness the Lord quietly and gently whispered to me, 'When you come to meet with Me, you have to come alone. Even when Ian was here, you still came to meet Me, alone'.

As I pondered those word, I had to agree, *Yes, He is right, Alone just the Lord and me.*

I was now able to face the morning and people. It was shortly after this that a special friend, Shona, rang. I told her about my early stroll in the garden with the Lord and the song.

'That song reminds me of another really, old song' she said. 'How does it go? Ah, yes, on the Jericho road ...' She continued singing. The song asks whether your load is too heavy and if so, give it to Jesus. It speaks of only room for two people on the Jericho road: Jesus and me; that Jesus is there always to help.

Yes, this was what the Lord had already told me this morning. Whether in the garden or on the road there is room for just Jesus and me. Yes, Jesus and me.

Deep within me came an assurance of the reality and presence of God anew which made me soar like an eagle above my circumstance and misery.

How many times had I glibly parroted off the words of songs without giving thought or affirmation to the words? However, these songs are now become part of my reality.

I can see how God wants to make the words of songs like this and the words of scripture real to me and to each of us. And How? By allowing hard times and trials into our lives. Like the trial I am facing just now. It's enormous, but my God is even bigger.

I cry, I hurt, I grieve – Of course. When I sing a song like, 'I Come to the Garden Alone,' I'm pulled up short with a jolt, like a horse reined to halt. I feel alone and abandoned. I see all the things we did together and all the plans – oh so many plans we had for our future, now gone.

I know the Word of God talks about how those who mourn will be comforted, about our sorrow turning into joy, about being victorious in all things, and I'm beginning to see that this is becoming my experience more and more. When I turn to the Lord, He is always there to meet me, and He takes the pain, the sorrow the burden away just as He says. He is more real to me now than ever before as I stand on His word and own it for my circumstance.

Father God and His Son, Jesus, are more than enough. Jesus' challenge, not just to me but to all of us, is 'Am I, my word, my presence enough?'

For your problems and difficulties which you are facing, this may not seem a practical answer, but in fact, it is precisely where you will find all your answers as I have found again today, in the garden, on the Jericho road, with Jesus.

Chapter 8

The Lord is My Shepherd; I Shall Not Want.

My three eldest sons and I were sitting around our dining table with the funeral director discussing arrangements for Ian's funeral. There had to be an autopsy on the body because the death happened in a paddock with only his son present. The local coroner was away, so the body was sent to Sydney, which caused a longer waiting period for release of the body. We decided on a date for the funeral, hoping it would provide enough time for this. We discussed flowers, pallbearers, the type of casket, notices for the paper.

It was all so mechanical. This was something that had to be done. I was present in body, listening, discussing details with the undertaker and making decisions with my sons, but I felt in a fog, unable to see clearly.

A short while after the Undertaker left, I noticed the three boys on the front veranda talking together, a quiet and secret gathering. I knew they were discussing the meeting we just had. I proceeded out the door to join them.

They stood watching me approach their huddle, discussions haltered. The funeral cost had been unmistakably missing in the meeting, obviously for a reason, but that had not escaped my notice. I was fairly sure the reason they were outside having their conference was exactly what I had been wondering. 'So, how much is it going to cost?' I came straight to the point. One of my sons told me the amount.

I was now coming out of the fog as emotion swept over me: was it a holy unction or rather a grief–stricken wife's vessel of sorrow receiving a jolt and spilling out its contents? 'What! That is so evil! How can it cost so much?' I had never had to deal with organising a funeral before. I had never thought about what has to happen or wonder how much it would cost. The fog had cleared but the temperature was rising. I never wanted this!

'Why should a grieving family have to pay out so much, putting an extra burden on them when they're already in a fragile state?'

My sons stood there taking the barrage. Their faces showed a mixture of emotions. Was it sadness, concern, embarrassment, sorrow themselves? They were sombre but also had concern and tenderness in their eyes. This was their mother. They too were hurting and hurting to see their mother like this. Fragile, oh yes!', they must have been thinking, 'that describes you very well Mum.'

My burning anger and grief, however, was preventing me from being sensitive to them. 'Why should it cost any money to leave this world? Dad and I would sometimes speak about this, and in the event of one of us dying we said we should dig a hole up the back in which to bury us.' I was hot, I was mad, and I was not happy.

My sons tried to explain what the costs included. 'There's the casket, the newspaper adverts, the flower arrangement ...' they continued, but it meant little to me.

Why was this such a sticking point to me? However, this was not the real thing that was bothering me. It was just one more thing, but it added to the hurt and pain I was feeling and gave a release for some of the emotions which I had kept under check while sitting around the table talking with an undertaker. 'Why can't we have a simple wooden box? That's what the Amish do. They make their own. After all, it's only the remains going into the box and then into the ground.'

Moments of pause: everyone was trying to digest the hard and awkward dish I was serving up. Joel, in such a gentle voice in comparison to mine, made a suggestion: 'Well, if that's what mum wants, why can't we organise a simple box made? That shouldn't be too hard. Can we look into it at least?'

After another pause digesting this odd suggestion, David added another view, 'Dad's family might think we were just being cheap and not honouring him if we did that.' More pausing, more chewing.

We were at an impasse. 'I think we should pray.'

In that prayer time, the Lord spoke so clearly to me that He was my provider. 'The Lord is my shepherd; I shall not want.' (Psalm 23:1) That is, not want for anything because I have all I need from Him. I thought about Ian's family. They would be horrified to think of their son, brother, uncle in a rough, handmade box. They would think it was cheap and that I did not think he was worth more.

I thought of my outburst, my lack of thinking of others, my lack of trusting God. I was convicted and humbled. With the prayer over, I apologised to the boys for my outburst and my lack of trusting God.

(Since then, the Lord has proved to me again and again that He is my provider. The only groceries I have bought since Ian's passing into glory are bread and milk. I have had donations paid into my bank account, so far totalling more than $15,000 and someone who doesn't even know me donated $1,000. I have a new washing machine. The printing of the order of service cost me nothing. Another person who has never met us gave me over $600 worth of school curriculum for the children.

I have people all over the world praying for the children and myself, most who don't even know us. On top of this, I have beautiful, sweet sleep every night, peace, unexplainable. My children play happily and sleep well.

Whenever I am feeling down, and things press in on me, I go to my saviour, Jesus, and He answers all my questions in unimaginable ways and fills my cup to overflowing. Through Him, I feel the closeness of Ian again. This is my God! This is Ian's God! This can be your God for there is no other true God.)

The Lord is my shepherd; I shall not want.

Chapter 9

Ian Willersdorf – Obituary Written by Himself

In April 2013 Ian was chosen to be a part of a men's 'Train the Trainer' course. As part of the preparation for the course, both he and I had to write our obituaries. Below is what Ian had written:

Ian was a man of his word.

He would do what he said that he was going to do. He would spend a lot of time looking at his calendar to ensure that he could fit everything in that was required of him. At times he found it hard to reconcile how people could say one thing and then not follow through.

Most of all, he was a Man of God's Word. He would quite often say about his work and to the people that he employed, 'You need to ask yourself, would Christ be happy with what you did today, because if not, then you need to evaluate why you are doing what you are doing.'

Ian gave his best. He was never satisfied with second best. That didn't mean that he had to be the best, he just had to do his best, and that is what he expected of others. That often meant being consistent, whether it was scanning sheep, shearing or traveling down the road.

In his relationship with the Lord, he would at times get disheartened because he felt that he failed the Lord. But Ian knew the promise of God: that for those who walk in the Lord, the Lord would be faithful to uphold and protect him. Ian was a leader himself but would not put himself forward as a leader.

Ian was passionate! He was passionate for the sheep that he worked with. He was passionate for his clients to be successful, and at times that was burden-full to him, especially in times of drought and hardship.

He was passionate for his employees to enjoy their work and become leaders. He tried to encourage them to be the best that they could be, both in their work and for the Lord.

He was passionate that young men would be men and tried to teach his sons and employees to be responsible and accountable. He had a saying that if you bark at cars and bite tyres, then you will end up getting run over. He did not like people making excuses for young men doing stupid things. If young men do stupid things, then they or someone else will end up getting hurt.

Ian was passionate about his family. While he worked hard and long, he would always be home ASAP to be with his wife, Julie and his family. He would try to spend time with the grandchildren and knew the importance of teaching them about the Lord. He built the business as he felt that he could train his children so that they would not be slaves to others.

However, he felt at times that he was a slave to his business until he gave the business to the Lord. This gave him more freedom to 'follow the Lord' the way he felt that he should.

With the workload, he was always trying to carry more than his share, and as he grew older, he still found it difficult not to do his share of the physical work.

Finally, he was passionate for his wife, Julie. Julie was the love of his life, his cherished wife and lover. While there were times when he let her carry more of the burden than he should have, he did try to be her protector and leader, encouraging her in the Word and her walk with the Lord.

The longer they spent together, the more they enjoyed each other's company. They both know that God has blessed them in many ways, one of them being the family that they were given.

But most of all, Ian knew that God was Lord and Saviour. And if you are not sure of your salvation or that you are going to heaven, then you need to reconcile with God. Be sure that you do not go to your grave without knowing the answer to the question that will be asked of you by the Lord, 'Do I know you?'

The song, 'A Man of His Word' by Bob Carlisle was a favourite of Ian's and sums up what Ian wrote concerning himself – Ian was a man of his word.

Chapter 10

Death Where Is Your Sting?
Grave Where Is Your Victory?

I feel lost somewhere in between now and then, reality and illusion. I am forced to live in reality, but all my feelings; my being wants to live in the illusion of Ian still being here. I go through the motions of normal living although much of it is unpalatable. Eating has no great appeal to me: a necessity to keep one alive. Life, death – so much depth to those words! Death has invaded my life bringing with it grief, tears, and numbness; squeezing out the joy of living.

The words of a song come to mind, 'Death where is your sting, grave where is your victory?' What do those words mean: death has no sting; the grave has no victory? *Haven't I been tasting, eating, living that sting?*

I look up John 11:25 where Jesus is talking about resurrection life, 'Jesus said to her, I am the resurrection and the life: he that believeth in me, though he were dead, **yet shall he live.** And whosoever liveth and believeth in me **shall never die.** Believest thou this?' (emphasis added)

'Believest thou this?' Jesus addresses the question to me.

Believest thou this? I ask myself. For Ian, yes! I can see that death had no sting because he did not actually die; he was already dead because he believed in Jesus. He was dead to self and to sin and alive to Christ. He just shed the outer coat (his physical death) and passed entirely through the veil into the very presence of God. And, I can say that I too am dead and have life forevermore and one day will be able to pass forever through the veil to face my Lord also.

Believest thou this? Yes, Ian has reached his destiny so for him I cannot be sad. He is home and in the most wonderful place anyone could ever want to be. However, I am still here feeling lost and abandoned.

Believest thou this? I want to believe, to answer 'yes' to Jesus' question to me.

I sense Jesus pushing me further. 'So in the nitty–gritty of everyday life are you going to let the grave, Ian's grave, have victory over you?'

'I want the pain, the sorrow, the sting I feel of my husband's death taken away, yes absolutely. But how?'

As I ask the question the Lord shows me again that there is someone who knows grief and sorrow far more than I. Isaiah 53:4–5 says, 'Surely, He hath borne our griefs, and carried our sorrows: yet we did esteem Him stricken, smitten of God, and afflicted. But he was wounded for our transgressions, he was bruised for our iniquities: the chastisement of our peace was upon him; and with his stripes, we are healed.'

There it is in Isaiah. I had never seen it before. 'Surely, He hath borne our griefs, and carried our sorrows...' Jesus carried not only my sin when on the cross, but also, amazingly, my grief and sorrow. He actually carried my grief and sorrow! That's 'carried' which is past tense. He took it upon Himself, experiencing the totality of it so I would not have to. Why would I want to try and carry grief when it has already been carried for me?

As I ponder these things, the Lord gives me much more of an understanding, a vision of the pain, the grief, the sorrow of Jesus on the cross. He experienced all my grief and sorrow which I now feel, as well as the grief and sorrow of people over all time. In comparison, my sting of grief and sorrow pales into insignificance. There is absolutely no comparison whatsoever.

'Oh Lord, dear Jesus, You have already experienced all this 'yuck' I'm going through, as well as sooo much more.'

Humility and awe surround me, and grief gives way to gratitude.

I have found the victory over the grave, over my husband's grave – at the foot of the cross and the truth of His Word; in quiet reverence of an awesome Saviour.

Chapter 11

He Is Not Here, He Is Risen

It was the 20th of December. My daughter, Michaela and my friend, Shona, who had arrived a week ago to help, were assisting me in deciding what to wear. I pulled a garment from the wardrobe. 'How about this one?'

'No, it's too plain. You have to wear something special.'

'Yes, and I don't want to wear black. I want something a bit colourful. It should be a celebration.'

What an odd scene it appears to be, one perhaps of choosing an outfit for a party rather than a funeral. 'I don't want people to wear black at my funeral,' I continued. 'I'd like to have some colourful scarfs or something that they can wear if they come in black. I need that written down somewhere, so people know what I want. Well, at least you two have heard me say it.'

Two more garments came out. I tried them on. Finally, we decided on the pale pink skirt with the ivory white cami and pink floral top, not too bright.

Today was the day. A lot had happened in the past ten days. I had even been to the wedding of one of our employees.

Two of my sons were groomsmen, one the best man. How bizarre – celebrating a wedding before the funeral of my husband?

It was 9:45. Everyone was ready. Butterflies were calling a meeting in my stomach as we made our way out to the cars. Paul, who was wearing a light blue shirt with pale stripes and tie, walked in front of me, opened the car door, and waited for me to get in. I took a deep breath and took my seat in the car. We travelled the eight kilometres to the Coolac cemetery. It was warm, no, hot, and promising to reach the forecasted forty degrees Celsius. The grass was no longer green – it had protested the lack of rain and was now dried out and dead.

As Paul opened my door, I again took a deep breath. With the climb out of the car was the venture into the next chapter in my life. A chapter that felt so strange – actually, it all had felt so strange and foreign to me. As I venture forward the undertaker's assistant greets me at the cemetery gate. My brother, Euan, who would be officiating at the service, also greeted me but with a hug. He had come down from Queensland and despite the hot weather was wearing a dark suit which contrasting with his grey hair.

A large group of people stood in the shade of the tree, a gazebo with fifteen or twenty plastic chairs had been set up in front of the grave, offering more shade. I've been to many funerals when I was the one standing waiting like these people now coming into focus. Now it is me! I am the one, the one they have been waiting for, the one they are looking so sorrowfully at, the one that is to sit under the gazebo. I breathe slowly, heavily, controlled.

As we make our way to the seats, I see brothers from Melbourne, from Sydney from Queensland. I see my sister from Brisbane, cousins from Victoria, Ian's mum and his brother and sisters, uncles and aunts. Seeing them all brings all those contained emotions to the foreground. I breathe slowly, in and out. My sister, Karen, ventures forward, as does my brothers and cousin Betty. We meet and hug, purposefully hug. I wipe tears, halting their descent. I breath, in and out.

We continue to the gazebo. In front of me lies the gaping hole nicely surrounded by fake grass–green mats, although fake, their pretence is a stark contrast to the deadness around us. Six of my sons, each wearing Akubra hats, wait at the back of the Hearse. They carry the coffin, three astride, with the lifeless body of my husband inside and place it hovering over the cavity.

We sit. A beautiful flower arrangement including proteas, which were a favourite of Ian, adorns the top of the casket. Beside it is a photo of Ian and a small soft toy, a sheep, a symbol of much of his work.

My brother, Euan, opens the service. He offers prayers and a short message. Children of the Wong family play music on keyboard, violin, cello, and flute. It sounds heavenly. I breath, in and out, this time more easily as the music flows over, around me.

Now Euan asks me to come forward. I have a message to share. A message of what God has been doing in this broken vessel, of putting broken pieces back, of teaching deep truths. With my notes in hand, another deep breath, and a resolution to share what God has been showing me I walk to the microphone which is shadowed by a big umbrella.

I can feel my heart racing, pounding, knocking, as if wanting to get out. I take another deep breath, in and out, and look at my notes. All eyes are upon me. The pause is pregnant.

With trepidation on my part and expectation from others, I begin. 'This is the fourth time I have been at this cemetery this week. I was here three days in a row; Monday, Tuesday, and Wednesday. Now here I am again today.' I focus on my notes. Breath!

'On Monday I came here with David (my second eldest son of twenty–nine years) to look at possible sites for the burial of my husband's body. We saw two possible sites and then wandered around looking at ancient graves; at newer ones; at graves of couples, multiple family members and of tiny babies.

As we were walking out the cemetery gate, I felt utterly sick in my stomach. The sick feeling continued into the evening. I asked the Lord what was this? (Of course, why wouldn't one feel sick to their stomach wondering in a cemetery deciding on where to bury their husband?)

I looked up some verses in the Bible and read: 'And as they were afraid, and bowed down their faces to the earth, they said unto them, why seek ye the living among the dead?' Luke 24:5

I felt the Lord's was saying to me, 'A cemetery is a place for the dead, not the living. It is not a place for you, Julie.' Amazingly the sick feeling which had still been with me left, and I was able to sleep well. God is so good!'

With the safety of my notes and the recollection of what I was reading, I feel a calmness come over me. I look up at the sea of people gathered, engrossed in what I am saying. I continue, 'The next day, Tuesday, I came with my eldest son, Luke. We met the pastor here at the cemetery and went on to Gundagai to talk to council regarding sites for graves. We returned to decide on the exact site. Again, we walked around looking at headstones: inscriptions in particular, to get some ideas for Ian's headstone. As we closed the gate upon leaving, I again felt sick to my stomach, and it continued till evening.

I decided to look again at those verses in the Bible. As I continued reading, the very next verse stated: 'He is not here, but is risen.' Luke 24:6

This time the Lord was saying to me, 'Why seek the living among the dead? It is not a place for you, Julie, and it is not a place for Ian. Ian is not here. He has risen!' Again, the sick feeling left me, and I slept peacefully yet again.' As I shared what the Lord had done for me, I continued to experience a calmness.

'Wednesday found Luke and me here again, this time meeting with a person from the council showing him the site we had chosen. We again wandered around looking at some more gravestones. As we closed the gate behind us, I felt normal, no sick feeling. Praise God! There was no way I could stop that gut–wrenching feeling from coming, and I could not get rid of it myself, but the Lord through His Word did.

Today I am here to tell you that Ian is not in this coffin, only his body. He is with the living God and our saviour, Jesus Christ. That is the power of the cross. Ian is not here he is risen!'

I had planned at this point to pick up some of the rose petals supplied and throw them in the air to show something of how I had felt after the ill feeling had left and the rejoicing which Ian now has. *Would I dare? Could I carry this out?*

I did not stand pondering too long. It was now or never. I picked up some of the rose petals and threw them in the air and said, 'For Ian, to live is Christ and to die is gain!'

As the service concluded, family and friends meshed their grief together with ours through hugs and tears. My unmarried children moved a short distance away and stood hugging one another. A dichotomy existed between the truth God had put within me to share and the emotions of grief we all felt. But this too was a part of the healing.

'For whether we live, we live unto the Lord; and whether we die, we die unto the Lord: whether we live, therefore, or die, we are the Lord's. For to this end Christ both died, and rose, and revived, that he might be Lord both of the dead and living.'
Romans 14:8–9

Chapter 12

The Thanksgiving Service

A thanksgiving service in the Yass memorial hall followed the family graveside funeral at Coolac cemetery. I had no idea how the ending of that day would play out. I am so thankful that God's grace is bigger than whatever comes our way.

Friends and church ladies from Yass had generously provided lunch in the Anglican Church hall for all the family members. Before going to the lunch, I ducked into the Memorial Hall to see if things had been set up, making sure Ian's photo was placed at the front. 'Oh Julie, we're so sorry about Ian.' I wasn't expecting anyone to be there. It was my pastor and his wife from a few years ago.

Seeing people for the first time brought the emotions, feelings, and reactions to the surface, which I had nicely wrapped together in order to do the next thing. I wiped tears away as we hugged, 'Terry, Beth. It's so good to see you. Thanks so much for coming.' We chatted further before I proceeded to the luncheon venue. As I went to pick up a plate,

I instinctively looked around the room as if trying to locate someone. My mind was playing tricks on me. I was looking for Ian. I bit my lip and looked up at the ceiling. *How do I do this? God, help me!* Part of me lives as if he were here while the other part was falling apart because he wasn't.

The day was a sweltering 38-40 degrees Celsius. The hall had no air conditioning. Pedestal fans were strategically placed to offer some relief from the pressing heat. They did little to reduce the heat but made it slightly more bearable having a breeze to evaporate some of the sweat forming on people's bodies.

The service began with prayer and then a favourite song of Ian's, 'Before the Throne of God'.

Ian's older sister, Jeanette, accompanied by his youngest sister, Tania, climbed the steps onto the stage and approached the lectern. Tania who was there for support, needed as much support herself as sorrow and heartache gripped at her, displaying glassy, tear weary eyes, clasped hands and a noticeable lump in her throat. Jeanette taking control of her emotions, however, spoke clearly, reading out anecdotes of Ian's life on behalf of his mother and siblings.

'He was a clean boy until he turned five ... He wasn't very accident prone himself as a child, he was the cause of a few accidents ... Ian also spent time trapping, dressing and selling rabbits to people in Kaniva ... a very competitive brother and sportsman always trying to beat any one of us at whatever we were doing ... he had the smelliest feet we knew of ... He was also quite a mischievous child and grew into a mischievous adult in many ways trying to catch someone out or play some kind of joke on them ... When we all became adults, he still impacted on us, this time with phone calls or visits ... we always knew when he was around. He could be loud and had a hearty laugh but could also be gentle and quiet.'

'Ian, our son and brother, will be sadly missed by all of us, but our memories and stories live on and we will see glimpses of Ian through his children and grandchildren as he has left many of his traits scattered throughout his nine sons, two daughters and eight grandchildren.'

Time was given for Ian's three oldest sons to share about their father. Luke, the eldest began. He was calmly in charge of his feelings as he read from his notes. 'From my earliest memories of Dad, I have always looked up to him as a man. He had both a strength and gentleness that I now appreciate more than ever. Whether it was disciplining us or rumbling on the floor tickling us, my Dad was a rock ... He was a man of integrity ... He was a man of passion ... He was a man of honour ... He had a presence, a charisma that made him a natural leader. And yet he was not proud. He is perhaps one of the most humble men I knew ... Most of all thank you for showing me Jesus. I love you. See you soon.'

Two other sons, Joel and David also shared words about their father, comforting one another as their words faltered.

My and Ian's brother-in-law, John Canaris had a close friendship with Ian and shared the same faith which is why he was asked to deliver the message. He shared some of the depth of that friendship and faith in a beautiful poem he wrote which he began and ended the message with.

"Ian, My Blood-Bought Child, Well Done!"

There was a man ... Ian – strong and true;
Serious, committed through and through.
His eyes were fixed; his gaze upon his goal;
Passionate, faithful, responsible, devoted was his soul.

God took this man, caught up without prior warning.
His duty done; his eternal Day now dawning.
With Jesus now; the fight is fought,
the course complete, his race now run.
God's Voice in heaven is heard ...
"Ian, My blood-bought child, well done!"

(Tribute to Ian Willersdorf, my dear friend and brother ... by John Canaris, Friday 20th, 2013)

Much of his message was based on 12:24 – "Except a corn of wheat fall into the ground and die, it abideth alone: but if it die, it bringeth forth much fruit." He brought out that even though a tragic and sad event, Ian's death as well as his life can bring about much goodness in the lives of his family and others, even though in the natural that may seem impossible. (Hopefully, this book, which would have otherwise not been written, may be one such thing). He also wanted to convey to all there the importance of responding in repentance and humility to the creator, an awesome and loving God who has so much goodness laid up for those who acknowledge the sacrifice Jesus paid for them.

Unfortunately, the message went for a longer than usual time and with the combination of a challenging and very long message, in scorching conditions, on such an emotional occasion became too much for a number of people and so walked out. I took it as being very disrespectful to Ian and his faith in God. Among those who walked out were some of Ian's family. I learnt later that with the length of time sitting on such a hot day had caused among these family members headaches to the point of vomiting and body aches, especially Ian's mum whose hip pain had become unbearable.

I sat watching as one family member then another got up and left, some in front of me, and not understanding all their reasons for exiting, I became more and more hurt and offended, thinking that if they were walking out on what was being said they were also walking out on what was the reason behind the goodness everyone had spoken about the man, Ian Willersdorf. In my mind I felt they were dishonouring not only God but Ian Willersdorf also.

I ended up being the only one remaining in the front seat, all on my own. So alone!

This was Ian's family! This should not happen; was not in the plan. God, why did You let this happen? Why did it have to be so hot? Why did John speak for so long? Why did they have to walk out? Why? Why? Why?

I had originally planned and written out something I was hoping to share at the thanksgiving service, but as the service had gone on and the hall so stifling hot, I was beginning to think better of it. However, now with the feeling of betrayal to me, to Ian and the Word of God, I felt I had to respond. Standing up, I motioned to Pastor Steve Maynard, leading the proceedings that I wished to speak. Full of emotion my feelings came flooding out; no, spewing out from the depths of my pain and sorrow.

'People can so easily honour Ian, my husband for the wonderful person he was, for the great things he did, how he stood out from the normal guy. However, when someone explains why he was like that, that it was God who was behind Ian's greatness, you don't want to know. Ian, himself, would acknowledge it was God, and yet you want to honour the man but not what he stood for.'

My eldest son, who came with me to the platform, whispered to me to have grace. *That would come after I first spoke my mind. Yes, then I would read my original piece.*

After it was all over, I felt confused. I lamented to God, 'I don't understand, and I wish things were different.' However, I knew I could not change it. 'You Lord, knew about all these things before they even happened, and You are in control.'

BELOVED

Chapter 13

No Water

It was the day after I officially said 'goodbye' to my husband at the graveside and then at the Yass Hall. The temperature was 40 degrees Celsius with a hot, northerly wind blowing. Yet another sweltering day. The heat was encircling me like a cloak which I wanted to take off but one I could not be free from. It was stifling.

The previous day we found the pump to the bore not working, which meant we had no water outside for the garden or animal troughs. As well, the dam was virtually dry due to all the hot weather we had been experiencing. The evaporative air conditioner did not seem to be working, blowing warm air rather than cool.

'You'd better turn the air con off,' my son David suggested. 'There's no water feeding into it because the bore pump's not working. That's why it's blowing hot. You'd be better off if you put the big fan which we use for shearing in the window. At least it will blow a heap of air around.'

With that suggestion, the fan was organized, which provide us with a blast of noisy, warm air filling our small lounge room. The room was adorned with a myriad of flower arrangements from well–wishers. They had been beautiful but were now looking rather limp and lifeless protesting how hot it was. We had an extra 25 people for lunch that day making 34 in total which added to the intensity of the day.

We were just about to start lunch when someone announced that the new washing machine which someone had graciously gifted us with was beeping and had stopped working. 'Oh no! Was it installed properly?' I did not need this today. More than the heat was encircling me now. 'I hope it's not broken. Did you take out the things to stop the drum moving when it travels?'

I left my sons to figure it out. 'The manual says this error means the machine's not filling with water. We've got everything connected up correctly.'

'Hang on. Check that other tap.' They found the real fault – the rainwater tanks were dry.

We live on a small farm in the country. Our drinking, washing, and showering water is all from rainwater tanks or the bore. Now we had no water inside or outside. Things weren't getting any better.

With limited water (we had two large water filter urns still with some water in) lunch was had, everyone fed, and most of the visitors left. Children were heading to the local pool to cool off. Thankfully, there was water on tap at the pool so we sent the pool–goers with every empty container we could find to fill with water.

While the children were cooling off at the pool, I wandered outside, alone, now in stark contrast to the throng of people who had more than filled my house. I walked slowly across the lawn to the fence, and it was there that things caught up with me. The heat was intense, pressing in on me. The thought of no water opened up more emotions as I looked to the parched dam and thought of the broken bore and empty tanks.

Oh, Lord! I have been here before many times – having little or no water. But God, why now? I just buried my husband yesterday in stifling hot weather; I had family members walk out on the service, leaving me sitting alone. Did this have to happen now?

The heat was not the only thing pressing in on me. I needed to go up onto my mountain.

I walked to the fence. What was that I could see?

Chapter 14

The Bird

It was a bird, but as I climbed through the fence, it flew away. What was this other thing now before me: a piece of bark; an animal of some sort? It was something standing motionless, erect, grey, and motley looking. As I slowly approached I saw that it was another bird, a young one. It was not moving and had its eyes closed.

Another bird joined the first one and together made a curious sound. I was quite close to the young bird, and as it opened its eyes and saw me, it started to flail about. I realised this was the baby and the other two, its parents. They were now making a somewhat frantic sound while flying to and from the baby and the tree. The fledgling appeared unable to fly and continued floundering.

Not able to rescue the situation, I moved away, wondering why I should even be witness to it. However, as I walked towards the dam, my gaze returned to the scenario: *Am I like that bird?* I continued up the hill and tried to sing the song, 'Come, and let us go up to the mountain of the Lord,' but my steps were slow and cumbersome, and so was my attempt at singing.

Several days earlier I had stridden up this hill (my mountain) to meet with the Lord singing that very song and upon reaching the top had a most beautiful worship time in the presence of the Lord and the most amazing feeling as if Ian was standing right beside me.

However, this day was different in all aspects of that previous day. I finally reached the top and slumped to the ground at the base of the big rock. As I thought about the glaring difference between those two days, I realised the question I had asked about me being like the baby bird was, in fact, affirmative: I was like that bird – helpless, unable to fly, floundering. Yes! That was me! *God, help me! How do I get out of this mess?*

'Look up!' Came the reply. I thought again of the bird. Its parents were up above, trying to indicate to him what to do. 'But how do I look up, Lord?'

'Look at what I did for you,' the Lord answered. I started to think again of what Jesus went through for me: the pain... the suffering... the anguish... the separation... the abandonment, the aloneness. Then I remembered the veil torn for me.

As my eyes lifted heavenward, to the dwelling place of God, I saw that my supposedly huge problem seemed insignificant now compared with what my Saviour went through for me. I felt so ashamed of my complaining, my lack of trust, and my focus only on me. As I acknowledged all this, there in the presence of the Lord, the words of scripture from Psalm 34:1 came to me: 'I will bless the Lord at all times. His praise shall continually be in my mouth.'

This was the same scripture I had read travelling home with Ian from Victoria on our last full day together. I had said to the Lord, 'I want this to be me.' He heard and now was doing it in and for me.

I stood up; hands lifted heavenward and started singing those words and kept on singing them over and over. 'I will bless the Lord at all times. His praise shall continually be in my mouth.' A miracle was happening!

Chapter 15

The Widow's Last Mite

I started down the hill, still singing the words of the Psalm, 'I will bless the Lord at all times. His praise shall continually be in my mouth.' As I descended my 'mount,' I noticed a car parked over the road in the neighbour's drive. I thought it was the neighbours themselves but soon realised it was someone pulled over with car trouble. I kept singing while continuing down the hill.

I need to go and see what is wrong, see if I can help them. I walked over the four-lane highway that passed our property and found out the vehicle had overheated and that this was not the first time that day since traveling 500km from Melbourne, but the third time. They were from Wollongong and had purchased this vehicle online, had flown to Melbourne and were driving it (or meant to be driving it) back home this day. It did not look good!

Being so hot, I offered to bring them to the house for a drink. The man poured the remainder of his bottle of water into the radiator, while steam spewed forth. 'I suppose we can, and we might as well fill our bottle with water.' *Oh! Water!* Gingerly I said 'Yes,' and we proceeded up to the house.

From the front window of my house one of my daughter–in–laws, Beck, looked out and saw a car pulled over and people walking up the drive holding a bottle in their hand, obviously wanting to fill it with water. 'Oh no!' she told Kylie, another daughter in law, 'It looks like they've got car trouble and need some water and mum is somewhere up the hill. What are we going to do? There is no water!'

As we approached the house, they saw I was one of the people, which now totally baffled them.

With not much time to explain I instructed the girls to serve our hot and weary guests some juice and keep them entertained while I desperately looked around for every available morsel of water in every conceivable water vessel – water filters, thermoses, drink bottles, even the overflow from the cool room. How excited I was to fill their container. I also managed to find a Bible, a tract, and a copy of the order of service from my husband's funeral the day before.

I gave them the Bible. They looked at each other and smiled. The curiosity must have shown on my face, as the husband explained, 'You see, my wife had a serious illness, and she was miraculously healed. I am a paramedic and knew it had to be a miracle of God. Since then, we've been attending church again.'

This brought a memory to my mind. 'God miraculously healed me too, from ovarian cysts some years ago. Then again, about a year ago, He healed me of chest pain. God challenged me at that time to surrender all to Jesus. This was not a new concept to me, but the Lord pointed out that surrendering meant my life, that of my husband and my children. As I was willing to do so, the pain left me. However, little did I know that the Lord would take me at His word because my husband died just ten days ago, with his funeral only yesterday.'

I handed them a copy of the service. Their eyebrows lifted slightly, and both stared at me intently with a mingled look of doubt and sympathy. No doubt I did not seem like someone who had just buried her husband. Addressing their shock, I explained, 'God has performed a miracle today. On top of my husband's death, we found out today that we ran out of water, and I was an abysmal mess. However, after meeting with the Lord on my mountain, He amazingly took my sorrow and filled me with joy.' I said this as I handed them their full bottle of water.

'Oh, no! We couldn't take it. You have no water.'

I continued to place the bottle in his hands. 'I insist. It's like the widow's last mite and it must be holy water and will surely get you home.'

Who could have believed that I would be doing this when only half an hour or so before I was in the depths of despair? What a miracle! What a mighty God we serve!

Chapter 16

Go To Sleep In Peace; God Is Awake

On my first Christmas day without Ian, I find an old journal entry. Below is that entry (note the date, less than one month before Ian's departure). 'If only I knew...'

November 19th, 2013
'Troubles are often the tools by which God fashions us for better things.'
−Henry Ward Beecher

   'Lord, my Lord' – 'to write these words and think upon them warms my heart. How amazing to be able to call you *my* Lord. Yet, I do not fully understand those words as I write about my current struggle. My soul screams out for understanding.
   The quote above speaks to me, and I know it to be true. However, I struggle with Ian and the older children being away so much, especially in the last two months. What gets to me is

that "work" appears to run our lives. What I mean by that is it seems to be the motivating force dictating what our family does. Many times we or at least some of us, have had to forego attending activities or events due to work.

The dilemma – we work to get money to live, and the nature of our business means the fellas have to chase the work which can take them far away. But do we need money to live? What a ridiculous question! Of course, we do, however, where in the Word of God does it say that? The Word says that we cannot serve God and mammon (money). In today's world we do need money to buy things. I think the problem is not in its use so much as our serving it and it controlling us, as the verse indicates. Is it our driving force?

All this extra work requiring Ian and the boys to be away has brought me frustration because it meant we could not attend things as a family. Recently in particular, not being able to catch up with friends from far away, attending a 21st, and a father–son/daughter camp. Also, with some of the older children being away, it meant they could not practice instruments with the other children for a concert which was coming up.

I am reminded of the verse in Psalm 68:19: 'Blessed be the Lord, who daily loads us with benefits.'

'Lord, it's hard to see all these things as benefits and to praise You when things to me don't seem in order. Oh, Lord, I am very weak.'

'Have courage for the great sorrows of life and have patience for the small ones ...Go to sleep in peace. God is awake!'
–Victor Hugo

'Lord, these things truly are like sorrows to me, and yet your words again come back to me. Words which I shared with someone on Sunday: 'In everything give thanks for this is the will of God in Christ Jesus concerning you.' I Thessalonians 5:18

'And yes! Lord, You are awake as the quote states. You know about all these things of which I have complained. You weren't asleep when they were happening. You daily load me with benefits, but I don't always see them, so help me to see and focus on those benefits. If my life is loaded with benefits, there is no room for anything else.
Benefits:

- Makes me aware of my lack of trust, showing me my need for God more.
- Makes me lean on You, my Lord, more.
- Enables me to grow in character.
- Challenges me to be a doer of the Word, not just a hearer.'

December 25th, 2013

Well, as I read that last entry, I can't help thinking, 'If only I knew'... I was struggling with Ian and the older boys being away so much, and the lack of family time altogether. They were sorrows to me then, but here today I have much, much more sorrow now that Ian is no longer here, never to return to me, never to be here for the children, never to lead the family. I thought back then was a hard place to be...

Oh, if only others may learn from my lesson! The children of Israel murmured in the wilderness. God continually forgave them as they turned back to Him, but they did not enter into their rest, the Promised Land. God hates murmuring and complaining. Wives, please thank God you *have* a husband!

Chapter 17

Christmas Day

Today is Christmas Day, the first without Ian, and just over two weeks since Ian passed from this life into God's presence. We spent the morning with my son, Joel, his wife, Beth, and their children. So lovely to be with family!

From there we went to have lunch with my mum at the nursing home where they provided a scrumptious Christmas fare for us. After we were full of Christmas pudding and read all the bon–bon jokes, my children entertained some of the residents with some instrumental songs. It was all very lovely. After coming home, I lay on the bed and dozed for a while before going to dinner with some friends in the evening.

On waking, my thoughts were filled with Ian. It was obvious that he was missing today. My eyes caught the photo on the dressing table, our wedding day. As I turned my head, the photo blue–tacked to the wardrobe door, our 25th wedding anniversary, beckoned me for attention. I thought about how Ian had brought that 'something else' to every situation; how he just 'made the difference'; how he made our family feel complete; how he brought the mundane to life with his jokes and antics; well, really with just his presence.

My thoughts continued. *Ian is no longer here to make the difference. How can I ever make the difference when I wasn't the one doing it in the past?* My future loomed ominously before me promising me no hope. It seemed to stretch before me like a menacing hand pointing forward to the cell of a convicted criminal. It was as if an unspoken voice somewhere, was declaring, 'This is your sentence!'

A feeling of despair and hopelessness washed over me, soaking into my being and finding some release only by forcing its way through tears. *How can I go forward without him?* A numbness crept over me and I remained on my bed for some time before finally dragging myself off the bed. We had been invited out for dinner.

The evening was spent with our good friends, the Wong family. The numbness lingered and I felt I was 'going through the motions'. We shared a meal and afterward joined around the piano, singing some songs. As the singing continued it became to me a healing balm. The music, the songs, the words were melting the numbness, enabling me to refocus my thoughts on the Lord and His faithfulness.

One of the songs which started the melting was 'My God is Near' by Mac Lynch. It speaks of knowing God's presence, especially when alone. How He knows our thoughts, our trials, and our pain; nothing is hidden from Him; He guides us, is faithful, and trustworthy so that we need never fear.
Yes, need never fear. That was it! Need never fear of facing the future without Ian; need never fear that I could not do it alone; need never fear of not being able to make the difference.

BELOVED

    Thank you, Lord, for songs and friends and fellowship, which helped put my thoughts in the right place.
    I never need to fear because God is always near!

Chapter 18

Delight Yourself in the Lord.
He Will Give You the Desires of Your Heart

My path crossed with Ian Willersdorf when his family moved into the district, buying and managing the local Post Office and General Store. His sister and I were in the same class, grade six, of a one–teacher school.

When I was 14 years of age, our paths not only crossed but also become some–what linked as we became attracted to one another. Our families both attended church, but Ian had never bowed his knee before the Lord Jesus. He was still lord of his own life and although not entirely enjoying it, drank with 'the boys', and smoked the odd cigarette.

My older sister acted as God's Holy Spirit, reminding me of what the Bible said concerning being unequally yoked. She even suggested another 'nice Christian boy' as an alternative. I did not want to know. But ... God would have His way.

One evening after reading my Bible, the still small voice of the Lord spoke to me, 'Julie. You have to choose between Ian and Me.'

I wanted to ignore the voice as I had done with my sister, but this was God.

No, Lord, surely not! Please don't ask this of me.

Again, the voice came. 'You have to choose between Ian and Me.'

That isn't fair! The battle ensued – the battle for my will or His will. I knew that in the end, I would have to choose God. That is why it was not fair. It was no choice at all. Even with my protest, deep within I knew I had to choose God and be willing to give up Ian.

God did His work first in me, then in Ian. I had intended to tell Ian that I had to call the relationship off and the reason why, but not long after my fight with God, Ian, while working alone on the tractor one evening, confessed himself a sinner and surrendered his life before God Almighty – just him and the Lord Jesus.

God is so awesome! I never had to give Ian up. I had been willing to surrender him to God, and yet God gave him back to me. Wow! God wants to be first in our lives, in everything, in every relationship, and then He takes care of the rest.

Delight yourself also in the Lord, and He shall give you the desires of your heart '–Psalm 37:4

Chapter 19
All To Jesus I Surrender

The Lord gave back to me the thing I most wanted, Ian Willersdorf, but I first had to be willing to give him up. We were married on April 14th, 1979. I was 18 years of age, Ian 20. For over 34 years we shared our lives together as husband and wife. We moved many times and lived in many different places. Ian's paid employment included farmhand/overseer, farm manager, shearer, computer business owner, accountant/company secretary, advisor to an IT company and owner of a livestock contracting business.

The Lord has blessed us with nine sons and two daughters over a span of 24 years. Those years have brought a mixture of fun and frustration, laughter and tears, joy and sorrow, but through it all, God has always been faithful. I have story upon story of God's faithfulness over my life: stories of miracles of healing in illness, peace in despair, and joy in the face of hopelessness. However, the most prominent trial and test I have ever had to face, began on the afternoon of December 9th, 2013. Unbeknown to me, though, God's hand had been preparing the stage for Ian's final act, the finish of his earth–bound race.

Looking back, I have been able to see that preparing, right back to that night long ago before we were married, when making the choice to give up Ian Willersdorf. The Lord also reminded me of a time a couple of years ago when at our annual home–school conference He challenged me to surrender all to Him: my life, my husband, and my children.

Around that time, I had been having a sharp pain in my chest sometimes even when lying in bed. It had been happening on and off for a month or so and then again at our home–schooling conference. I was lying in bed, and with every breath, I had a sharp stabbing pain in my chest. I told Ian that morning for the first time, and with the speaking it out realised that I had tremendous fear ... *What was this? What did this mean?*

The previous day I heard a friend's very moving, emotional, and challenging story of how she nearly died of typhoid overseas in a remote area. She had to come to the point of surrendering her life, and that of her husband and children, and being willing to never see her children and husband again on this earth. There wasn't a dry eye in the room, for with the telling came the emotions pulling on our own heart strings as we contemplated ourselves in the same scenario. Now, as I felt the fear in my heart, those strings were pulled tighter. *Yes, what did this mean?*

The next day on the last day of the conference we were informed by the worship leader that he changed what was originally planned and instead chose the song 'All to Jesus I surrender, all to Him I freely give'. As we began to sing the song, the words struck me anew, and I struggled with what they were saying. The words were jumping off the screen and racing towards me, grabbing me, choking me.

All to Jesus I surrender, all to Him I freely give. *Freely surrender all my life? God You must be joking? After the testimony I heard yesterday?* What was God asking of me? My mind was racing from my stabbing pains to the emotion-filled testimony and then to the song. *Oh God!* As I tried to sing the song, my throat tightened, that emotional string pulling tighter. The words were too hard to swallow. *Me, surrender ALL to Jesus?* The Lord was pinpointing what the 'all' meant— my life, my husband's life, my children's lives.

Lord, I thought I was your follower; thought I had surrendered my life, but why am I finding this so hard?

Part of me knew what it means to follow Jesus, to surrender absolutely everything, but it's one thing to say it and another thing to do it. I couldn't escape; couldn't pretend. My eyes filled with tears, overflowing down my cheeks.

I felt He was asking me to be willing to say goodbye to those I loved so dearly, to be willing to face death and part from my loved ones. With trembling and still more tears, remembering my friend's story, I surrendered it all to God. ALL to Jesus I surrender.

Amazingly the pain left and has never returned. Praise the Lord! BUT... I have had to say goodbye to my husband. God took me at my word. I had freely surrendered Ian to the Lord, firstly before we were even married, but He gave Him back to me, and then again at that conference. God took me at my word and chose to take Ian, but He has honoured my willingness by supplying an abundance of amazing grace for this present trial.

Should I then be angry and bitter for no longer having the years Ian and I were still expecting to have? We had plans for the future, but hadn't I surrendered Ian to God? Hadn't I so long ago been willing to never marry Ian? Shouldn't I be grateful for God allowing me to marry him and for any years at all that we spent together, let alone over 34 years; 34 years never promised to me?

We can so easily make commitments to God, surrender our lives, our things to Him, and yet not fully understanding what we are saying. We so easily say we trust God, and yet when trials come, our response can often display our lack of trust.

All to Jesus I surrender – What a challenge!

Chapter 20

God Prepared the Way

I can see now how the Lord went before us in advance of Ian's sudden departure from this world. I was reading the words from John 10:3–4, and it reminded me how the Lord is like a shepherd who calls his sheep by name and leads them by going before them.

'... and He calleth His own sheep by name and leadeth them out. And when He putteth forth His own sheep, He goeth before them, and the sheep follow Him: for they know His voice.'

What wonderful words! He goes before His sheep. Although Ian's death was a tragedy and a total shock, I can look back and see the hand of God going before us and preparing us for such a calamity and heartbreak. Let me share some of those things with you.

David, our second eldest son, had always worked in the business with Ian until offered another job which, after a couple of years, ended in July 2013. He came back to work in the business just five months before Ian passed away. During those months he was able to relearn the ropes and gain a rapport again with clients.

But more than this, when Ian collapsed that fateful day, David was the one with him. That too, was unusual as David was usually in charge of his own team while one of the younger brothers or younger sister would generally have been with Ian – not this day of all days.

Earlier in 2013, Ian had written letters of encouragement to each of his eleven children, to his mother, to his three daughters–in–law and to me. What a precious keepsake!

Ian was to take me away for a weekend. He was able to fit it in around work and combined it with seeing our eldest son and his family with their new baby. It happened just three weeks before his passing into glory.

Our annual home–schooling conference is in January each year – not that year. It was changed to early December to fit in with the speakers' schedules. It was the first and only time the conference was in December. This meant that a lot of our home–school friends were able to see Ian only a week before he passed away, which had a tremendous impact on them.

After the conference, we went to Kaniva, Victoria, where Ian's mum lives, and stayed with her for a few days. The children perform in a concert there each year. On the day before Ian departed from us, his mother got to see and hug him (we live over eight hours away). Later, in recalling that moment, she said he gave her the biggest hug – what a sweet memory for her. His brother and one of his sisters also were able to see him at that time.

The night before he left us, Ian and I were sitting together on the couch, children all in bed after a big day's traveling home from Victoria. Our daughter, Michaela, came out and sat with us and proceeded to ask Ian what he thought about some ideas for her future. She was tired after the day's travelling and had been in bed. She had the persistent thought to talk with her dad about the ideas which had been navigating through her mind.

Those thoughts finally drove her from her bedcovers to come and talk with us. She was not aware that after that night her Dad would never be here to ask his opinion on anything. Usually Ian would discuss such things with me before answering but instead said, 'Well, just off the top of my head and without talking with Mum about it, this is what I think ...' She got her answer the night before he left us. How good is our God?

On the very morning, before God took Ian into His presence forever, he was driving off to work after saying goodbye but then stopped. Curious to see why, I went out the front door and saw he was moving a sprinkler. He could have just got back into the vehicle and continued driving out the gate, but instead, he saw me and proceeded up the front steps to kiss me goodbye. That is the last time I saw him and what a sweet memory.

Chapter 21

The Letter

In the weeks following Ian's thanksgiving service, I felt I needed to write a letter to Ian's siblings. Why? I wanted to let them know that I forgave them for what they did in walking out on Ian's memorial service, to ask them for forgiveness and I felt I needed to let them know just how much they had hurt me. After all, I thought, how could they appreciate my forgiveness unless they knew how much they had hurt me? I was perhaps rather deceived in my motives.

I drafted the first letter (the first of seven in total) and showed it to one of my older sons. A few changes later, I was able to show it to another son who brought about a few more changes. I then e-mailed it to a third son who suggested still a few more changes. He also asked me what my intent for sending the letter was.

Ah! What was my intent indeed?
I assured him of my good intentions. After some more changes and then showing the letter to two more friends with again

some helpful comments, the question came up again, 'What is your purpose in writing the letter?'

God was getting to me. Was I deceiving myself? Was it really to show my forgiveness or to let them know how much they hurt me?

Let me share with you some of that first letter:

"... I was struggling last Friday, as one by one many of Ian's family walked out, many in front of me. I have heard reasons since, from some, but was I not hot too?

I deeply apologise for the length of the message on such a hot day. I take full responsibility because I didn't give John a time limit and I should have. Please forgive me. But please, can your hearts be so cold that you could not think of me, the one most affected by Ian's death, watching as family walked out, dishonouring Ian and myself. I ended up all alone in the front seat – all alone! In case you didn't notice. Did anyone in their discomfort give a thought for the one grieving the most? Did any of you have the heart to think of anyone but yourself and your discomfort? Yes, someone did. One person felt my aloneness and came and sat with me. That was the greatest kindness of love shown to me. I have forgiven you all,"

I have forgiven you all! Really? Is this forgiveness, true forgiveness? What truly is the intent of this letter? How shameful it is to have to own up to this. Does this show the wonderful forgiveness of God seen in the death of His only Son; or the love and forgiveness shown by the prodigal son's father when his wayward son returned home? (This story is in Luke chapter 15). Did the father let the son know all the pain he had caused him, the sleepless nights worrying, the torment of not knowing if he was alive or dead and the grief of thinking he might be dead? No, not a word of all that.

What sort of forgiveness was I offering? Indeed not what is pointed out in chapter three of Colossians, "Forbearing one another, and forgiving one another, if any man have a quarrel against **any**: even as Christ forgave you, **so also do ye**." What was Jesus' example that we are also to do? "Father forgive them for they know not what they do", were the words He uttered after they had nailed Him to the cross; He who was totally innocent.

And what does the Lord's prayer say? Forgive us our sins, as we forgive others. In other words, Father God, forgive me as much as I am willing to forgive other people.

God over those couple of weeks dealt with my true motives and my idea of forgiveness, enabling me to truly forgive those whom I had felt hurt and offended from. Following is the last draft of that same portion of the letter:

'Regarding the thanksgiving service, I want to clear the air: I was hurt watching as family left, but that is all behind me, and I hold nothing against any of you. I know you were suffering too and so I deeply apologise for the length of the message on such a hot day and for the offence it caused. John Canaris was not only a brother-in-law to Ian but also a friend, and he knew and shared Ian's faith and wanted to portray some of that in his message but could have in a much shorter length of time. I take full responsibility because I did not give John a time limit. I did not know he was going to speak for such a length of time. Please, please will you forgive me?'

What was the outcome of the letter? One of Ian's sisters wrote, 'Dear Julie, I am touched and humbled by the attachments and would not change a thing. I know the family united.'

Not too long after sending this letter, we were able to attend a 40th birthday party for Ian's youngest sister where all his family was present. It was there that his mother apologised and asked me to forgive her. I know that on the day of Ian's thanksgiving service she had been struggling physically for sitting so long with a painful hip. I assured her that I had already forgiven her and that there was no longer anything to forgive. Before we left, she wanted a photo of her immediate family but insisted that I was also to be in the picture, which was echoed by her children. Wow! When we humble ourselves before God and seek His way, His love, and His forgiveness, this is what one letter can do.

'And all things are of God, who has reconciled Himself by Jesus Christ and has given to us the ministry of reconciliation.'
– 2 Corinthians 5:18

Chapter 22

Blessed is He that Considers the Poor

In January I was visiting friends with my family. My sons offered to come and help them on their property to get away from it all and have a break. It was a change from the 'usual' and working with friends makes it enjoyable. The work helped to keep them from mulling, and the fellowship with friends is like a healing balm.

It is such a blessing to stay in their lovely granny flat with some of my children, giving us some privacy. This morning I read Psalm 41, and the first two verses caused me to stop. It was the phrase, 'and keep him alive,' which got my attention. At one time I would have just glossed over those words without a thought, but today they pulled me up abruptly.

'Blessed is he that considereth the poor: the LORD will deliver him in time of trouble. The LORD will preserve him *and keep him alive*; and he shall be blessed upon the earth: and thou wilt not deliver him unto the will of his enemies.' (emphasis added) Psalm 41:1–2

My thoughts turned to Ian (as if that was unusual). When two are joined together and then pulled apart, there is a ripping, a tearing, bleeding which needs to be stopped. How can only one half live?

I read the words 'and keep him alive.' *Yes, that's what I wanted: for Ian to be kept alive, to be alive!* Then as I reread the verse, my mind entered into a struggle.

The Lord will preserve and keep alive those who consider the poor. *Didn't Ian consider the poor? He can't have, as he was not delivered in his time of trouble. He died! The Lord didn't keep him alive. Many people I know have lived much longer than Ian has, and many who definitely do not consider the poor. How can I reconcile what God is saying here?*

As I sat pondering this, the Lord began to unfold and remind me what being alive actually is. You see, Ian didn't die on Dec 9th, he died long before that and so did I (see Rom 6). Also, God made us alive in Him through Christ's resurrection, and He has kept us alive, living that life eternal, now.

The scripture in verse two goes on to say, 'He shall be blessed upon the earth.' Ian is not physically on the earth now, but those who knew and loved Ian continue to bless him upon the earth as they see the heritage he has left within each of his children. Ian is still being blessed as any of his children receive praise, awards, or accolades.

Today I also read in Luke 24:51–53, 'And it came to pass, while he blessed them, he was parted from them and carried up into heaven. And they worshipped him and returned to Jerusalem with great joy: And were continually in the temple, praising and blessing God.'

Previously, Jesus' crucifixion and death made His disciples grief–stricken, scared, and depressed. They were lost without Him – I can so relate to them. Here He is about to leave them again, for good, to abandon them after sharing so much together over the previous three years. However, we find no sadness this time.

Instead, we find just the opposite – Great joy filled the disciples, and they gave praise to God in the temple and blessed Him continually. Wow! The difference in their response to those two events is astounding. The first one left them with no hope because they did not understand what Jesus had been trying to tell them.

With His second departure from them, they now understood – Jesus was the giver of life itself. Death could not hold Him, and He had won the victory that now belonged to the disciples too. They knew that although Jesus in the flesh was departing from them, Jesus in Spirit would not only be with them but in them, always.

The same should be true for us, for me. The Word says that the disciples were continually praising God in the temple. The Bible also refers to our body, individually and corporately, as a temple, the temple of God's Holy Spirit. Thus, we too, like the disciples, should be continually praising God in our temple, within ourselves.

'I will bless the Lord at all times. His praise shall continually be in my mouth'. The verse from Psalm 34:1 continues to hunt me down. That day before Ian was carried up into heaven, I said that I wanted it to become a reality in my life: blessing and praising the Lord no matter what. The Lord takes us at our word. His Word chased after me and found me. He got my attention. A person of praise is what I want to be, and He has shown me the way yet again.

I began my readings this morning having questions which weighed down my soul with sorrow, but the Lord changed all that by revealing this astounding truth to me from His Word.

Chapter 23

Life without Ian

It has now been six weeks of life without Ian. 'Lord, as I think about the number of years living without Ian physically by my side; thinking about my life and my future without him, it brings a thick cloud of doom which menacingly hovers over me, pressing heavily down upon me.'

My thoughts turn to my mother, who lived without her husband for so long (30 years) and as I imagine that same 'so long' living without that special someone in my future, it becomes abhorrent to me. The taste of it is bitter. It repulses me! *I don't want it!* I protest. It is unwelcome!

But yet I can't stay here stuck in a moment that has already passed. Time does not wait; it marches on. I have no choice. I do not even know if I will be here tomorrow to have a 'so long.' My times are in your hands, Lord.'
I consider these charged emotions and gloomy thoughts; I see that they are self–pity. 'It's not your way, Lord. You want me to think of others, not wallow in self. Jesus, you did not come to this earth to serve yourself, and I am to have the same mind

as you. Your word says to think of others as more important than myself.' *That is definitely not me naturally.*

'But let this mind be in you which was also in Christ Jesus: Who being in the form of God, thought it not robbery to be equal with God: but made himself of no reputation, and took upon Him the form of a servant. 'Phil 2:5–7

'Lord, You want me to see the needs and hurts of others; to breathe life into them – Your life into every relationship. Then I can truly live and be free from the oppressive clouds.' Three nights later...

'Lord, another hot night.' I pull back the doona and crawl into the bed. Alone. In the past, this has often been a common occurrence for me. Ian was often away with work, and I would frequently retire for the evening, alone. Then it was temporary; now it is permanent. I balk at those words, *alone* and *permanent.* I do not want to know them as they loom menacingly as a truth I will face every single night. Despite my protest, they cling to me. No, not just cling, they are a part of me.

Despite the stark reality that I now face life without my husband, without Ian, I am comforted by the what the Word of God says, that I am not alone. I have always lost arguments with the truth of God's Word.

As I remember the promise in His word, He speaks to me ever so softly, 'I will never leave you or forsake you. You are not alone. I am with you always, permanently.' The Lord of life, the God of all comfort, the God eternal, has spoken and promised NEVER to leave or forsake me. These are no longer mere words. These are becoming a part of me.

From under my bed covers, I am able to say, 'You, Lord have always been with me. You were with me whenever Ian was away with work. Not only are You forever with me now, but You are my comfort, my strength, my shield, my friend, my counsellor, my provider, my all in all.'

Chapter 24

Alone!

Alone! What a thought, what a feeling. We can be alone in a house full of children, on a crowded bus, at a football game or even at a family gathering. Life is not meant to be lived 'alone.'

What is life anyway? Jesus said, 'I am the way, the truth, and the life.' True life is found through and in Jesus. Another time Jesus said, 'I have come that they might have life and that they might have it more abundantly.' John 10:10

Jesus is the giver of life but if your life and purpose for living depends on and is found in your partner or your marriage or anything or anyone else, then disappointment and grief will be the result if it ends, and your life would fall apart. However, if one's life and purpose is found in the living God who never changes and promises never to leave you or forsake you, then you will never be disappointed no matter what happens in this life. It sounds easy in theory.

The Word of God is true from the beginning, and the enemy wants to speak lies by using my senses and feelings, like in the original garden, to bring me undone. I have a choice to believe God's word or believe my feelings. I choose to believe God's word: even though I am alone regarding not having a husband, I have a relationship with the living God who is always with me, who loves me unconditionally, who protects and sustains me and provides my every need.

My husband could not do all that for me. It is through drawing closer to God in a loving, trusting relationship, seeing God as my all in all, that I can feel an even greater and more complete oneness in Spirit with Ian than before. How can that be? I can't explain it, but now I do have a special connection with heaven.

So, ... alone? No, I am not alone! I lay on the couch on the front of veranda pondering these things, and words from the Bible speak truth to me: How could I possibly be alone when I have a husband who loves me perfectly, unselfishly? I have a husband who cherishes me and who never leaves me... who never leaves me.

I have a most loving father who is there whenever I need him and showers me with good gifts. I also have a teacher who is constantly showing me new things. I have a counsellor for when everything gets too much for me, a brother who knows everything about me, and I have a wonderful friend who sticks closer than a brother. To top it off I have a Shepherd who protects me and lovingly cares for me.

Statements of faith – taking God at His Word:

A Husband to the widow: 'For thy Maker is thine *husband*; the Lord of hosts is His name.' Isaiah 34:5b

A Father: 'Every good gift and every perfect gift is from above and cometh down from the *Father* of lights' James 1:17

The Comforter: 'But the Comforter, which is the Holy Ghost, whom the Father will send in my name, He shall *teach* you all things.' John 14:26

The Counsellor: 'For unto us a child is born, unto us, a son is given: and the government shall be upon His shoulder, and His name shall be called Wonderful *Counsellor*...' Isaiah 9:6

A Brother: 'For whosoever does the will of God, he is my *brother* and *sister* and mother.' Mark 3:35

A Friend: 'Henceforth I call you not servants ... but I have called you *friends*.' John 15:15
'... and there is a *friend* that sticketh closer than a brother.' Proverbs 18:24

A Shepherd: 'I am the good *shepherd* and know my sheep and am known of mine.' John 10:14
'For as he thinketh in his heart, so he is.' Proverbs 23:7
(emphasis added)

Chapter 25

That Special Someone

'Lord, walking up the hill this morning, the thought struck me again that even though I have the children to spend time with, I am alone. I spent time last night talking with my sons, Paul and Raphael about their week, but the reality is I face life alone as the parent, the head of the family.' The feelings of aloneness and responsibility again swept over me in a very tangible way. *Why do they follow me and hound me?* I try to escape them, outrun them, but when I think I am finally free; unexpectedly, they pounce on me and coerce me till I submit to their pressure.

Aloneness! As I continued up the hill, I thought of those who are unmarried and the loneliness they too feel not having a spouse; a soul–mate, someone with which to share their life. Ian and I were married young, he was 20, and I was 18. Being single for a long time, waiting and hoping for that 'special someone' to come along has not been a part of my thoughts or experience. Now, however, I can feel something of their yearnings and loneliness.

More thoughts ran across my mind. *Until you have tasted something, you don't know what it tastes like or what you could be missing out on.* This thought caused me to remember a time years ago while living near Tamworth. We were hoping to purchase a house and had prayed about the particulars we wanted. After looking at many houses, we finally found one with everything we had talked and prayed about and even more we hadn't thought about. We also found out that the owners were Christians who were so pleased we were looking at their house. We thought that this was the house for us. Everything was so right. 'Thank You Lord!'

As it turned out, we never bought the house, never got to live in it. At the time, I could not understand why the circumstances that unfolded meant this 'dream house' was not for us. Why would God show us the house we had asked Him for and then not allow us to buy it?

Little did I know that we would only live at Tamworth for another nine months before Ian's job took us south, closer to Canberra. How much harder would it have been to leave the house of our dreams after nine months than to leave the rented house? I did not know all that, but God did.

I reached the top of the hill and rested against the big rock to catch my breath. How much harder is it to be alone after sharing your life intimately with a spouse for over 34 years, having and raising 11 children together, than if you had never had that special 'someone.' 'It's hard to let go and move on, but with You Lord it's possible.'

Instead of focussing on my aloneness and missing my special man, I can be glad of the 34 years we spent together. Now it only seems like 34 wonderful years. Any bad or bitter parts don't matter and fade away into insignificance. It's interesting how perspective changes.

Chapter 26

Jehovah Jireh, My Provider

The Lord is so amazing! He continues to help and sustain us in many ways often without our knowledge at the time. As a family, we look back and see God's hand preparing us for Ian's leaving us, and now as we continue forward, we see Him provide our every need materially, emotionally and spiritually.

I still have no death certificate and found out it could be weeks away, which makes it hard to sort life insurance, other legal matters, and financial things. However, in the past two weeks or so, the Lord has been reminding me that He is my provider.

As I was travelling through Victoria, I received a call. I recognized the number so pulled over to take the call. 'Hello, this is Jenny from Centre–link. Could I speak with Julie Willersdorf please?'

'Yes, this is Julie.'

'I want to talk with you about your Centre–link payments: in regards to being a director of Noble Management.

Because you are a director, any profit from the business is seen as part of your income which will affect your future payments. I need you to send me some reports from the business regarding the profits.'

'But I don't ever draw any money from the business.' I couldn't see how money I have never had could be some of my income.

She continued, 'It doesn't matter whether you draw any of the profit or not, because you are a director you are entitled to it and it is counted as income.'

While still on the phone, I felt a rush of emotion: confusion at first, followed by anger, frustration, and exasperation. *How ridiculous! Being a small family business, I have never drawn upon the profits of the business as that would put more pressure on it if I did. How could that be my income when I've never had it as income? I don't even draw a wage from the business, let alone the profits. How can they do this to me?*

Some of this seeped into the conversation, but not wanting to spew it all down the phone line, it sat under the surface, like lava waiting to erupt through the surface of a volcano. With the phone call finished I remained sitting in the car by the side of the road. With the emotional volcano still simmering, I was unable to continue my journey.

I sat pondering the information I had just received lamenting the injustice of it all. I clenched my fists. I wanted to punch out at something, anything, to scream at the unfairness. I took some deep breaths and thankfully, in that moment, the Lord broke through the turbulence with that still small voice.

'I am Jehovah Jireh, your provider. If I so choose to use Centre–link to provide for you, I will, but I am the one to provide how I see fit. You are not to look to the world's way of doing things. You are not to trust in Centre–link or the world's system but to trust in Me.'

He had gotten my attention, and peace washed over me as He stilled the turmoil and took my frustration. 'OK, Lord! Of course, You are my provider.' I had forgotten that truth so quickly. It's easy to say God is my provider but not so easy to actually believe it and put it into action in everyday circumstances. His grace was there to help me. The turmoil had subsided. There was no longer any lava to flow.

I turned the key, the motor ticked over. I resumed my journey confident in my saviour, my provider.

I had already forgotten this lesson, so the Lord wanted to make the reality of Him as my provider something I really understood. So, on Sunday, God proved it to me yet again. After our church service, a lady from another Church came to see me. She offered her condolences, 'I'm sorry to hear of your husband's death. I wanted to send you a card but thought you may not know who I was, so I decided to come and see you in person.'

It was true, I had only met her once or twice before and had forgotten her name. 'I wanted to help in some way,' she continued producing an envelope from her bag and handing it to me. 'I want you to have this.'

Taking the envelope, I thanked her and assured her of how good the Lord has been to me. How He has provided for me and been there for me whenever I felt down by taking away my grief and sorrow.

Later upon opening the envelope, I found it had a cheque for $500. Praise the Lord!

'You are Jehovah Jireh, my provider.'

Chapter 27

Trust Me

God had made it so clear over the past two weeks that He will provide for me. I am a slow learner and during this week, I had that very thing tested. Did I really believe God is my provider?

The test came as someone I know rang to see how I was and asked if Ian had had life insurance.

'Yes,' I replied, 'but I can't access that because they haven't been able to determine a cause of death which I need for the life insurance, and because I'm the sole director now of Noble Management they take all profits as part of my income,' I replied.

'We just want to make sure you're being looked after, and no one is cheating you out of anything owed to you. We've got some ideas that may be able to help you.' At first they asked me to pray about it as they offered their advice.

'You know the best thing to do is to go bankrupt and/or sell off all your assets to your sons, then they can start another business in lieu of the bankrupt one.' I wasn't sure about this bankrupt thing, and it must have shown in my voice and the pregnant pauses as they tried to assure me this was not illegal, 'This is normal business practice. You don't need to feel guilty about going bankrupt. Have you lodged your tax yet?'

'Actually, no. I'm still waiting for the accountant to get back to me.'

'That's perfect. You can get the accountant to write it into the figures.' *Was this God's way of doing things?* I could not help but think back to when we were in terrible debt to the Tax Office and had given the business to the Lord. We purposed to make all business dealings and decisions according to His word and His way of doing things. What was now being presented to me did not sound quite right.

By the end of the phone call there was no more talk about praying about it. 'Did you understand all I've said? I also know someone experienced in all this who could answer all your questions and help you with this. He even helps all the Alan Bond type people.'

I came off the phone a little confused as it all fitted with the fact that I didn't have the death certificate and that the tax was not yet lodged, but I had an uneasy feeling about it all. *I'm sure this isn't God's way!*

They had said to me this is fighting against the unfair world's system of being cheated from what is rightfully mine. I still had an uneasy feeling but hadn't the time to take it to the Lord and think through it clearly as it was just before the busy pre–dinner time. I rang a friend that evening. Straight away she confirmed my feelings that this was not what God would want.

The next day I found a book in my cleaning up called The Tax Solution – 100% legal secrets to reduce tax. I thought,

'How uncanny is that?' and set it aside to look at. Today I took it, my Bible, and a notebook up onto my mountain. After looking through it (not understanding half of it) and spending time with the Lord, I knew the book and the advice from the phone call were not for me.

The Lord's still small voice came to me again, 'I am your provider not just in finances but in all things. Look to Me. Trust Me to lead you in the way you are to go.'

Praise the Lord! He wants a living, personal relationship with us all, having a simple, child–like, trusting faith that He is a good, good Father.

'And my God shall supply all your need according to His riches in glory by Christ Jesus.' Philippians 4:19

Chapter 28

Ian's Birthday

Today is the date of Ian's birthday, February 16, 2014. He would have been 55 today. With this thought, emotions rise from within expressing itself in thought: *That is not fair!*

The thought of Ian never again having a birthday on this earth seems too much to ever ponder. The thought of Ian, his memory, stuck at 54 while I continue to get older and continue to live life without him is distasteful to me. The thought of leaving him behind repulses me. *I don't want this! I didn't ask for this!* I feel stuck. Stuck somewhere between living now and living then, with my foot firmly on the brake, making sure I go no further into the future but unable to turn around and stay in the past.

As I think about my own father's death and Ian's father's death; the years which have passed, diminishing my thoughts about them – I don't want that to happen with Ian. My mind and heart protest! I love him!! I don't want to stop loving him. I don't want to forget him or think about him less and less and less and less.

BELOVED

    And yet, I can't go back, can't rewind, can't unravel what has happened.

Today on your birthday,
My darling, I love you ever so much!
Oh, God! You took my husband;
Oh, God! It makes me sad.
That our life together
Is no more.
Why did You take him from me?
You so wanted him with You.
I too want him here,
Beside me.
But...
Not my will, but Thine Oh Lord.

Chapter 29

*Unless You Eat My Flesh
and Drink My Blood*

My Bible reading for the day was John 6:53–58. Then Jesus said unto them, verily, verily, I say unto you, except ye eat the flesh of the Son of man, and drink his blood, ye have no life in you. Whoso eateth my flesh, and drinketh my blood, hath eternal life; and I will raise him up at the last day.'

This was an unusual and hard saying for the listeners of Jesus. What was He talking about, eating his flesh and drinking His blood? Is this cannibalism or Satanic worship?

The reading continues, 'For my flesh is meat indeed, and my blood is drink indeed. He that eateth my flesh, and drinketh my blood, dwelleth in me, and I in him. As the living Father hath sent me, and I live by the Father: so he that eateth me, even he shall live by me. This is that bread which came down from heaven: not as your fathers did eat manna and are dead: he that eateth of this bread shall live forever.'

The Word goes on in verse 66 to say that 'From that time many of His disciples went back and walked no more with Him.' Eating Jesus' flesh and drinking His blood! Truly a hard saying! Notice too, it was not just anyone who turned back, but many of his disciples.

So, what did Jesus mean? I decided to look deeper, particularly, verse 57. '*As* the living Father hath sent me, and I live by the Father: *so* he that eateth me, even he shall live by me.' With the use of the words *as* and *so* this seems to me to be like an equation.

$A + B = C + D$

[The living Father sent me (Jesus)] being 'A' + [I (Jesus) live by the Father] being 'B' =*(so)* [he that eateth me (Jesus)], 'C' + [he shall live by me (Jesus)], 'D'

I can see some similarity here between 'Jesus lives by the Father' and 'we live by Jesus' (B and D in the equation above) and thus 'the living Father sending Jesus' and 'we eating of Jesus' should be very much the same also (A and C).

Jesus living by the Father 'B', meant He was to trust the Father for absolutely everything and to do what the Father wanted, giving up His own will in preference to the Father's will. Similarly, we are to live by Jesus, 'D', doing what He wants and giving up our own will in preference to His, to live by Him only. He becomes Lord, Master, Director, King of our life.

'The living Father sent Me', 'A' – the Father sent Jesus to die for sinful mankind, for the ungodly, to free us from the trap of sin and death. If eating Jesus flesh, 'C', was synonymous with the Father sending the Son, then it takes on a whole new meaning to what I had thought. It would seem to mean that we too need to be willing to give up our life and even die for the ungodly.

This indeed is a hard saying. No wonder many of Jesus' disciples turned back from following Him. Paul in Romans says that perhaps some, a few, would be willing to die for a righteous man and even for just a good man. He gives the impression no one would be willing to die for an ungodly man. He goes on to say that Jesus did just that: died for the ungodly, us, while we were still sinners. He calls us to follow Him, just like the fishermen on the lake with their nets and the tax collector, collecting and counting his money. 'Come, follow me. Go where I go, do what I do.'

As I ponder all this from today's reading, I ask myself, 'Am I willing to die, give up my life for anyone let alone for the ungodly? Willing to die for those who reject the existence of God and laugh away the seriousness of rejecting Him?' Where was God taking me with this reading today?

Chapter 30

Living By Jesus

This new understanding of these verses was too close to home due to the scenario laid out before me. A few days previous someone I knew was jokingly saying he did not mind going where it's hot because he enjoys a good BBQ, knowing my beliefs about heaven and hell. He had joked about this on other occasions. This particular time he wouldn't make eye contact with me. These jokes about God and hell had reached exasperation point in my still grieving state of mind. I had had enough!

I felt like responding but kept my mouth tightly shut though it didn't stop my thoughts. *You know what I believe about God, and if that's what you want, then you can go to hell. I really don't care!* It was only a thought, but I knew it was a stinking attitude, and I knew it was wrong, but I could not do anything about it as my feelings were fresh and raw and overpowering me.

That was the other day, but after the Bible reading from John 6 about eating of Jesus' flesh I now had a choice before me. Continue in such a rotten attitude and join the disciples who went back and walked no more with Jesus because it was too hard a saying, or submit my will to His, being willing to not only forgive this person but be willing to die for him.

'Surely you don't mean for me to literally die for him? Literally! That would mean my children would be not only fatherless but also motherless. Who, anyway would I be willing to die for and leave my children orphans? Is there really anyone I would do that for, and yet You're asking me to do it for him, for him of all people.'

'I love him!' came the reply. 'Hell was not made for man. I desire all to be saved.'

A huge battle began. I had in the past surrendered my life, my children, my husband to the Lord and now I have no husband. I cannot glibly say yes without understanding I have to be willing for God to take me and leave my children parentless.

'Let this mind be in you, which was also in Christ Jesus: who, being in the form of God, thought it not robbery to be equal with God: But made himself of no reputation, and took upon him the form of a servant, and was made in the likeness of men: And being found in fashion as a man, he humbled himself, and *became obedient unto death, even the death of the cross.'* Phil 2:5–8 (emphasis added)

After days and days of struggle, I found myself about to take communion during the church service. Suddenly it took on a new and a far deeper meaning. 'That the Lord Jesus the same night in which he was betrayed took bread: and when he had given thanks, he brake it, and said, 'Take, eat: this is my body, which is broken for you: this do in remembrance of me."' (1 Cor 11.24)

His body was broken for me. Does 'this do' mean just to break this small token of bread in my hand like He broke bread? Is that the 'do this' or the 'Follow Me' He asks of me? Or is it rather, 'as you remember what I have done for you, do the same: be broken for others, be willing to go to the cross, to die for others, to die for the ungodly?'

It was as if the Lord was speaking to me, 'Unless you eat my flesh and drink my blood, you have no life in you.' Again, came the question in my mind, *was I going to be like those who turned back? ALL to Jesus I surrender? Hadn't I said this to the Lord already? Didn't I really mean it then? All!*

I could not partake of this communion bread unless I were willing to follow; to 'do this.' My hands were shaking; tears rolled down my cheeks. My throat was tight, 'Lord, I don't want to turn back. If this is what You require of me . . . then not my will but Yours be done.'

The willingness to surrender brought about the miracle needed. Now that I was broken and crushed, my attitude towards the person changed and in less than two weeks, I had the opportunity to publicly honour the person in question. Our eyes met and we hugged without any feelings of hurt or disdain. Praise be to God! Jesus came to reconcile us back to God and to each other.

'Whoso eateth My flesh and drinketh My blood hath eternal life.' This I now know is living by Jesus.

Chapter 31

Renewing Wedding Vows

Back on September 9th, 2012, Ian and I, along with another couple, renewed our wedding vows during the church service. In weeks previous we had attended a marriage seminar which impacted us both, and our marriage. So, when Marriage Sunday was approaching, and our pastor gave the invitation of renewing of vows, Ian decided we would renew ours.

One thing particularly from the seminar which challenged us, was how our marriages should share the Gospel message with those around us. The way we relate to each other in our marriage should show forth how Christ relates to His bride. Also, our marriages speak not only to family and close friends, but also to those watching on at a distance.

The husband should portray the role of Christ in sacrificially loving His bride, and the wife should respond as the church should to a wonderful, loving saviour. As husbands and wives we all fall short of this, but this should be our goal as it is what marriage was made for: to glorify God.

The conference speaker continued to say that a married couple may speak forth the gospel stronger than anyone delivering a sermon. Whether we realise it or not our marriages are in fact preaching to those around us. The question posed to us was, 'What gospel is your marriage preaching?' *Hmm, that's a good question!*

We, as married people, can impact this world amazingly by how we treat and respond to our spouse. With so many marriages falling apart and sadly, so many Christian marriages, it is no wonder that the whole meaning of marriage is under attack and challenged.

Ian and I started to see our marriage in a new light. As we submitted more to God and sought to apply what we learnt, He took our marriage relationship to a whole new level. Ian and I were growing in love with each other more and more. We wanted to renew our vows because of our new and deeper understanding of marriage and how it was impacting our relationship.

We wanted our vows to portray some of what we now understood of marriage and our life together. Below is a copy of the vows Ian made to me.

'I, Ian, acknowledge you, Julie, as my one and only wedded wife. With joy I proclaim the commitment of my life to you that together we may be one, offering God our bodies as living sacrifices that we may bring glory and honour to Him. As is Christ to His body, the church, so I will be to you a loving and faithful husband who willingly serves. Always will I perform my headship over you even as Christ does over me, knowing that His Lordship over me is one of the holiest desires for my life.

I promise you my deepest love, as I seek to love my Lord; my fullest devotion as I devote myself wholly to my Lord, and my tenderest care as one who is the shepherd of my soul. I promise I will live first unto God rather than others or even you. I promise that I will lead our lives into a life of faith and hope in Christ Jesus and in the same way to disciple our children who God has graciously blessed us with, ever honouring God's guidance by His spirit through the Word; that together we may accomplish God's work to advance His kingdom.

So, throughout life, no matter what may lie ahead of us, I pledge to you my life as a loving and faithful husband, being heirs together of the grace of life.'

Chapter 32

No Matter What May Lay Ahead

The vows I made to Ian are below.

'I, Julie, acknowledge you, Ian, to be my one and only wedded husband. With joy, I proclaim the commitment of my life to you. As you have pledged to me your life and love, so I too acknowledge my love to and for you. My life is not my own, I have been bought with the precious blood of Jesus, my Lord, and as I submit myself to Him, trusting in His Lordship, so I willingly and wholly submit myself under you as my husband that together our marriage may proclaim the Gospel to those about us.

As I seek to love, honour, obey and please the Lord so will I love, honour, obey you, ever seeking to please you. God has prepared me especially for you to strengthen, help, comfort, and encourage you as your help mate working together to accomplish God's work to advance His kingdom. I thank God for the blessing of eleven children and seven grandchildren thus far, and commit to discipling them together with you.

Throughout life, no matter what may be ahead of us, I pledge to you my life as an obedient and faithful wife, being heirs together in the grace of life.'

As I read through these vows what hit me were the words, 'No matter what may lay ahead,' and 'Commit to discipling them (our children) together with you.' None of us know what may lie ahead and I certainly did not know what lay ahead for me when I made those vows. Now it definitely does not include discipling the children together with Ian. Now it's just me. *Oh, that is huge!* Just four words but within them is a life being lived, struggling, questioning, striving.

In revisiting these vows, I felt the weight of now being a single mum. *Is there a day that passes without me feeling that weight?* Mostly life keeps going and so do I. It's the times of struggle with a particular child or the clash of siblings or when I pause from the busyness to see the lack of input from a husband and father that the weight becomes too heavy.

I want to climb out from under its mass, to rid myself of the burden, to find freedom from its encumbrance and walk back into the land of my vows. Single parent was never a part of what I saw as my life. That was always someone else. Someone I pitied and someone with whom I could not relate to. But there was no escaping, single parent was now not only a title but a part of me.

Reading these vows also took me back to revisit some words written by Helen Steiner Rice which Ian and I recited together on our wedding day on April 14th, 1979. It ministered to me. especially in the last verse where it says, 'A love that is endless and never can die but finds its fulfilment with You in the sky.'

As I pondered the words of that poem, I thought the best thing a husband can do for his wife is what Ian said when renewing our wedding vows: 'I promise that I will lead our lives into a life of faith and hope in Christ Jesus.' When we find our life and hope in Jesus, then the love we have for each other comes from above, in His love for us. That is what lasts eternally.

If we had not had that in our marriage, I would not have that eternal perspective and my life would have little hope now, without Ian here. Now, however, I have a love that is endless and never can die.

Chapter 33

I Just Want To Be ...

It's March 5th, and I find myself on the floor, head in hands, tears rolling down my face. *This is all too hard!*

I have just finished with a call from the tax office – the payment plan for the business' debt had defaulted. This was due to an additional tax amount, unknown to me, not paid on time. After the initial shock of the default, I was able to organise with them a new payment plan with an up–front sum of $3,000 paid next week and $1,000 per week from then on with a total of $18,000 debt still to pay. With having to pay workers compensation insurance and BAS of $21,000 there has been no extra money to put aside. I didn't need this today.

Why today in particular? Everyone, including me, are just recovering from a violent and extremely infectious gastro bug. One son vomited on the bedroom carpet overnight but did not clean it up or tell anyone, so it sat there all day and the next night. Especially considering the hot weather we have had, when I discovered it, the smell was not good. I have scrubbed and shampooed three times and also used eucalyptus, vinegar, and bicarb soda but the smell continues to persist.

I am still trying to organise a decent school routine in between dealing with coroners and others concerning Ian's death certificate due to there being no cause of death on it. I need this to claim Ian's superannuation and life insurance. Forms have to be filled out for the insurance, and with Ian's passing, two of my sons have to be made directors of the business. I am the one who pays the bills, talks with the tax office, manages the finances and bank balances, pays employees, tries to run a farm and tend a garden as well as run a household of 10 people. Oh, then earlier this week the big chest freezer stopped working. We found out only after everything had thawed – a whole other story.

Today I asked the children, the four at home, to weed the garden while I was talking on the phone to the tax office. After the long call had finished, I found them playing Lego in a bedroom with school–books not put away, bedrooms a mess, and weeding not done.

I can't cope with all of this!

It feels like more than plates atop sticks which I have to keep spinning; instead, the plates are full of food which I cannot keep spinning and one after another topples spilling food everywhere, and I am left standing, or rather sitting in the mess, holding sticks with no plates on top.

I feel like giving up!

As I sat on the floor in tears feeling totally overwhelmed, I recalled another time, some 22 years previous, when we ran a small business while having three young children. As I slammed the office door shut, I said to Ian, 'I've had enough! I just wanted to be a wife and mother.'

So, again I just want to be a ... wife?   Well, a mother at least. That thought pulled me up abruptly.

That is a big part of my problem – I am no longer a wife; I no longer have a husband. I can see why I am in such a mess, why my circumstances have undone me, but it brings me no answer, only despair. Ian, who was the managing director of our business, who knew all about farming, who had the voice of command, and who could take some of the load off me is no longer here and never to be here again.

What door have I to slam this time and to whom can I say that I just want to simply be a stay–at–home mum without having to sort out all this other stuff? I would then have more time for my children, for teaching and training them, for working together, having fun together, enjoying life together.

As I have been writing I feel the Lord answering me, 'I am your husband now.' This was no imagination. When the Lord speaks there is power. Those words coming from the Lord of Life flow through my whole being, bringing truth and dispelling the lies and lack of hope. Again, I am changed.

That means I am a wife! – The Lord continues, 'Take My yoke upon you and learn from Me, for My yoke is easy, and My burden is light.'

I do have a husband, the Lord Himself, who will not just take some of my burdens but will take all of them and substitute it for His, which He assures me is not heavy at all but light.

"Thank you, Lord,' I say rather weakly, for heaviness though lifted from me, still hangs with a threatening presence over me as I close my eyes to sleep.

Chapter 34

Thy Maker is Thy Husband

The next day some of the previous day's heaviness still hovered over me. *I need it to be real: that You are my husband!*

The Lord directed me to Isaiah 54: 'Fear not; for thou shalt not be ashamed: neither be thou confounded; for thou shalt not be put to shame: for thou shalt forget the shame of thy youth, and shalt not remember the reproach of thy widowhood anymore. *For thy Maker is thine husband; the LORD of hosts is his name*; and thy Redeemer the Holy One of Israel; The God of the whole earth shall he be called.' – Isaiah 54:4–5 (emphasis added)

WOW! Then I came to verse 13 – 'And all thy children shall be taught of the Lord; and great shall be the peace of thy children.' Again, the words washed over me: all thy children shall be taught of the Lord. It brought truth and restored hope. *Thank you, Lord!*

My eyes jumped down to verses 14 & 17: 'In righteousness shalt thou be established: thou shalt be far from oppression; for thou shalt not fear: and from terror; for it shall not come near thee. No weapon that is formed against thee shall prosper; and every tongue that shall rise against thee in judgment thou shalt condemn. This is the heritage of the servants of the Lord, and their righteousness is of me, saith the Lord.'

The Lord shall teach my children, and I shall be far from oppression and fear. What a word to bring me Lord! It is real! You are making it real! I see more clearly now. You as my husband directed me this morning to read Proverbs 6 with the children instead of our normal reading of the Psalms. I thought it was just me choosing Proverbs instead of Psalms, but You directed my choice. Verse 20 read, 'My son, keep thy father's commandment and forsake not the law of thy mother.'

Just a few nights earlier we read those same words, but it was in Proverbs 1:8. I was surprised to see it come up again in today's reading but in a different verse. I said to the children that God must be trying to get our attention and teach us this particular thing: Keeping their father's commandment and not forsaking their mother's law. In other words, keeping or obeying what I say.

This led me to share, rather emotionally with the children, all the stresses coming upon me; how by them not obeying my law or my words, adds to that stress. 'That phone call yesterday was from the Tax office letting me know that the payment plan for the debt the business owes defaulted and now we owe them even more money. I asked you to go out and weed the garden as the phone call was taking a long time. Instead, you disregarded what I said which goes against what God is saying in this reading.' The children were attentive but some not looking directly at me.

'Dad would normally be here to help sort this out as well as all the things to do with the farm. I still have things to sort out to do with Dad's death certificate as well. Children, I don't need you to make things harder for me by not obeying me.' My throat tightened; my voice was wobbly. I tried to stop the tears from forming. My youngest child got up from his chair and came and sat next to me. The child on my other side put his arms around me. Both rested their heads on my shoulders. Faltering I continued, 'I need you to help me by obeying, by easing the burden, not adding to it.' Tears were welling up in more than one pair of eyes.

There we sat letting it all sink in: my children being challenged; me a mess; my children comforting me; me comforting them.

Now I find in your word how You, Lord, as my husband will teach all my children. Here it was happening without me even being aware of it. Thank you, Lord! You are making it real.

Chapter 35

My Cross To Bear

Today, March 30th we sang a song at our church's worship service which spoke about bowing to God and laying everything before Him. This afternoon I told the children we should be careful singing these words unless we mean them. The scripture from Matthew 15:8 came to mind, 'This people draweth nigh unto me with their mouth, and honoureth me with *their* lips; but their heart is far from me.' If we sing words about laying everything before God, we need to do it; lay everything, our goals, our dreams, our friends, our pastimes, etc. all down at the foot of the cross. Otherwise, we are no different to the people Jesus spoke about.

A few things had upset one of the children earlier in the afternoon, and they were harbouring a not–so–pretty attitude. They seemed particularly challenged by this. However, as the afternoon continued, they seemed to make themselves scarce.

I lay on my bed after preparing the evening meal, and I thought how often it all seems too much for me: the everyday necessities of washing, cleaning, cooking, the schooling, the garden, the farm, and the business. *And now Attitudes!* I sigh deeply. On top of all the necessities is the sorting out of attitudes in and amongst the children.

Sometimes when Ian was away, I would experience similar feelings. Feelings of being so overwhelmed that I needed my emotional tank filled up before I could cope with those of the children's. My release was letting off steam to Ian either, over the phone, or once he came home. Just having him there as a listening ear, someone who knew me and who knew the situation helped me.

Well, Ian's not coming home, and I can't phone him. 'Lord, even though I know You are in total control and it was Your plan for Ian to enter into Your eternal presence, I still have contrary thoughts running through my mind; like a child wanting something he hasn't got.' *I want Ian here, not there*! Intense emotions rise from deep within my soul to unite with those wayward thoughts.

Many times over the years I have felt overwhelmed and hard done by with Ian being away due to work. I have often wrongly compared my situation with others and wished things were different. It felt like a burden I had to bear. I often thought I was stretching to snapping point. Now all that comes back cloaked with resentment, ungratefulness, and complaining. I protest: *I thought to bear the cross of having my husband so often away from the family and from me due to work, was quite enough to carry without him now gone forever. It seems so unfair!* Raw emotion comes spewing from my mouth: *It seems so unfair!!*

Was it to God I was complaining or was I just letting the pressure control loosen? I am stuck in this flood of emotion, thoughts pounding wildly like waves in a storm. *I need a way*

out. I need to swim to the shore, to safety but I can't. I need saving!
So, I turn to the Saviour.

'Lord, this is the reality of my feelings just now, even though I know You do all things well and for my good, I still wish Ian were here; I still question You. My feelings are very real. I know I am not to trust or follow them. I know Your Word is true and real, but I need for You and Your Word to be more real than my feelings.'

I turned to a devotion book and read this quote, 'I would rather walk in the dark with God than to go alone in the light.' –Marg Gardiner Brainard

My thoughts were refocusing. *Walking in the dark for me just now is the departure of Ian. Yes, it can feel oh so dark! On the other hand, having Ian here would be to me, walking in the light. How good that would be and yet, this quote states we can go alone in the light, the implication is alone without God.*

Having Ian here meant I could so easily turn to him for advice, for counsel, for love and comfort more than looking to the Lord as the provider of these things. Now that I can no longer turn to Ian for those things I have to look to the Lord.

Why did it have to take such a dark tragedy to make me more aware of the Lord in my life? That is often the way it is. We get busy with our lives and complacent with God, so that it often takes a shock, a darkness, to make us realise we really need Him, or need Him more.

Often the way is burdened and dark for me, but amazingly there is becoming a keener sense of God's presence felt. I am beginning to understand that 'I would rather walk in the dark with God than to go alone in the light.'

'Praise be to You, oh Lord! All glory is due to Your name! Again, You have rescued me from myself in my overwhelming sorrow.'

'Give unto the Lord, o ye mighty, give unto the Lord glory and strength. Give unto the Lord the glory due unto his name: worship the Lord in the beauty of holiness.' – Psalm 29:1–2

Chapter 36

I Will Glory In My Weakness

I read a quote from Horace Bushnell this morning: 'Trust God for great things, With your five loaves and two fishes, He will show you a way to feed thousands.'

It seems, at times, I can barely feed myself, let alone thousands! I often feel overwhelmed and burdened without Ian here so that trusting God is hard enough let alone trusting Him for great things. Yet His Word reminds me that when I am weak, He can make me strong.

'Without You Lord, I can do nothing, but with You, I can do all things, so your Word says. So, with Your help, I will try to say with the apostle Paul, 'I will glory in my weakness,' for without a husband, not only do I feel weak but often helpless and alone.'

Roy Hessin in his book, 'God Cares for You' says the following:
God is present with you. He is the God who is there – Jehovah Shammah. His presence in you is the hope of your life, the

peace of your mind and the song of your heart. His presence means that it is well with your soul. He desires to be the centre of who you are and all you do. Where would we be without Him?'

I cannot begin to imagine where I would be without Him. I need to read this over and over until I really know it– Jehovah Shammah: The God who is always present, always with me, desiring to be at the centre of who I am. Yes, always with me. Then I can sing the words, 'It Is Well with My Soul' from my heart.

I know that is what You, Lord, are trying to teach me: to be immersed in who you are. Then when I understand how great You are, I will have no trouble trusting You for great things. I will glory in my weakness because when I know I am weak and can't do it, You can do it through me and then thousands will be no problem to feed.

Taking me at my word the Lord directed me to read verse 10 from Isaiah:
'Fear thou not, for I am with thee;
Be not dismayed, for I am your God.
I will strengthen thee,
Yea, I will help thee.
I will uphold thee with the right hand of
My righteousness

'Oh, Lord, You are so wonderful, so amazing! I am in such awe of You! To think that You would love me so much to want to commune with me and I with You, to speak so precisely to my situation. I feel so humbled and so unworthy.

When I think about who You are, my mind cannot grasp it all; that you know every bird, every ant, and the number of hairs on everyone's head. How can that be? It is inconceivable for my understanding; unbelievable! To see the stars, unable to count the number of them, how can I imagine or understand Your immense greatness, You, the one who made each star? In comparison, I am nothing, and yet You sent Your son to this world, for me, Your creation. How amazing!

Lord, I fall so short. My mind goes back over all the years I have known You and desired to follow You, and I feel I have not gone far from when I first started. You are so long-suffering with me.

Oh, that I might truly know You and the power of Your resurrection; that I may no longer live; that Christ may live in me; that I might glory in my weakness so You can be strong in me.'

Chapter 37

Your Arrows Stick Fast in Me

Last week I read Psalms 38, I particularly noted verses 1 and 2. 'O Lord, rebuke me not in thy wrath neither chasten me in thy hot displeasure for *thine arrows stick fast in me* and thy hand presseth me sore.' – Ps 38:1,2 (emphasis added)

Little did I realise that these words would play out in my life in the days which followed. This came in the form of contrary words spoken, and e-mails received which felt like sharp arrows penetrating and wounding me. My thoughts swirled, unchecked and offences were taken; I felt pressed down by a heavy weight; I was drowning in a sea of negative thoughts; an ocean of self-pity. All this had the effect of making me physically ill with flu-like symptoms.

I know that nothing comes into my life without the Lord knowing and He even permits the arrows and fiery darts of the enemy to come. The psalmist even dares to upset our nicely formulated theology by claiming the arrows are God's: '*Thine arrows stick fast in me.*'

God is in control and knows what we are going through. However, the current of life's busyness easily sweeps this understanding away. I think I am on track and doing fine, but I so easily cut short my time with the Lord or forget it due to more 'pressing' things. My armour perhaps isn't in place… and then the arrows come. And they did come, thick and fast.

I prised the first one out, but before I knew it, another came with another quickly following, and still another. I was sore and bleeding from the first arrow. My wounds were bad. How could I escape? It was too much for me, emotionally and now physically.

I was so unwell the next morning as we set off for my nephew's wedding in Melbourne, 5 hours away, that I let Benjamin, my 16-year-old son, drive who was on L-plates. He was not actually invited, but there was no way I could drive on my own. My sinuses ached, my nose was blocked, and my eyes heavy, so I slept for much of the first half of the trip. It was wet and raining heavily, and I remember looking up at one time as Benjamin was passing a truck with another just in front of us. I was jolted awake; with the realisation he was only an L plate driver. What else I had missed?

That night I tossed and turned. The arrows, the offenses had penetrated and poisoned my sleep. However, the Lord was trying to show me the way to deliverance and healing. 'Seek My face.' I heard, but I was so trapped in the offenses I struggled to look up. As sleep continued to evade me, and the Lord's words continued to draw me, slowly I yielded and sought the Lord Jesus. As I did, He showed me my sin of taking offence when He, the creator God, took no offence when his created beings treated him with scorn and nailed him to a tree. It was there at the foot of the cross He humbled me and showed me my lack of trust in Him and His Word by my complaining.

As I calmly, boldly, and humbly passed through the veil, His flesh, into the presence of God and bowed before Him my answer came. He delivered me from my negative thoughts, of taking offence and I was able to sleep. The next day I attended the wedding with little or no symptoms. Praise the Lord!

The Lord is so good. He promises to be with us and to even answer before we call. Knowing my pathetic state, He provided me with the answer. Now in this morning's Bible reading, Psalm 76, I can see clearly the victory played out. I read how the Lord breaks the arrows of the enemy. That means the Lord makes these arrows of cutting words, offences, and negative thoughts ineffective.

Not only does it mention the arrows broken but also the shield, sword, and the whole battle. 'In Judah is God known: His name is great in Israel. In Salem also is His tabernacle and His dwelling place is Zion. *There brake He the arrows of the bow, the shield and the sword, and the battle*. Psalm 76:1–3 (emphasis added). Wow, the whole battle and that is what He did for me. No wonder the Psalmist says in the same chapter that the Lord's name is great and excellent and that 'the wrath of man shall praise Thee.' Psalm 76:10

As I delve further into this reading and ask the question, 'Where was this battle destroyed?' In Judah, it says; in Israel; in Salem; in Zion, His dwelling place where God dwells with His people and where His people dwell with Him. In my situation, when did my deliverance come? After thrashing about with my thoughts and finally bringing them before the Lord. My deliverance came from Zion, from going to the Lord.

Psalms 77:3 says, 'I complained, and my spirit was overwhelmed.' This is what was happening to me. I let situations and thoughts turn to complaining. This is why God says to give thanks in all things because complaining only overwhelms us. And it had surely overwhelmed me.

Later in Psalms 77, it says, 'Thy way, O God, is in the sanctuary; Who is so great a god as our God?' My answer to the oppression of the past week I found in the sanctuary, through the veil where God dwells. It is there that we see 'Thou art the God that doest wonders: Thou hast declared thy strength among the people.'

Who is so great a god as our God, the one true God and Jesus Christ His son?

Chapter 38

Seek My Face

When I had those arrows of offences coming at me which rendered me very ill, the Lord was saying to me, 'Julie, look into my face.' It is amazing how a few simple words can cause such a reaction. I had been tossing and turning instead of sleeping when He spoke those words to me.

'Look into your face? I have not been able to bring Ian's face to my mind once since his passing. When I close my eyes to picture him nothing comes up. I wake from sleep with no dreams of Ian. His face I cannot see, and You say to me to 'Look into Your face.' How can I see Your face, to look into it when I can't even picture my husband's face?'

The emotions, the flesh did not want to yield. *I've been here before, how many times? Fighting between you and Your ways and me and what I want. You are God and who am I? Oh, that I might seek You with my whole heart! Yes, this is the cry of my heart.*

I knew in my heart that looking to Jesus, looking into His face was, in fact, my answer to all those arrows (problems and offences). Initially, I could not see how it could happen. However, that began to change as I focused on coming into His presence.

Hebrews 10:19–22 speaks about that. It says we are to come boldly into the holiest place by the blood of Jesus, through the veil. The picture here is of the holy of holies in Solomon's temple where no one could enter except the High Priest and then only once each year. That place was where the very presence of God dwelt. During Jesus' crucifixion, the curtain over the entrance to that holiest place tore in half from top to bottom, symbolising that the way into God's presence is now available by His spilt blood and through the torn veil.

Hebrews goes on to say that this veil is Jesus' flesh ... the suffering Jesus went through for us was as if His flesh was literally torn in two, like that veil and like the bread at Communion. We, in order to come into God's presence, need to picture ourselves walking through the veil, the torn body of Jesus.

So, as Hebrews states that we can come boldly into His presence, in my mind I do just that but, as I begin to walk through that veil, I realize this is no ordinary curtain but flesh and blood, this is Jesus' body. This is what happened to Him whilst on the cross. As I continue to make my way through this veil, thinking about the cross, the tearing apart which sin, my sin did; Son from Father, I now see myself splattered with blood, Jesus' innocent blood. How could anyone freely choose to walk through such a veil without feeling the weight of guilt upon them? Jesus' blood upon me proclaims me guilty. It was my sin which took Him to the cross.

I then fall down as I see the evidence of my sin against Jesus, against Father God: His blood splattered all over me. My sin, my taking offence, my complaining, added to the pain, the grief, the sorrow, and the agony of Jesus on the cross and that is why He cried out, 'My God, My God, why have You forsaken Me?' – Matthew 27:46

'Oh, to see the pain, written on Your face... Oh to see my name written in Your wounds', as the song, The Power of the Cross goes. As this became my focus, I again felt deeply, the enormity of my current sin and guilt in contributing to the death of Jesus. What I had been offended over (which caused those arrows to stick fast in me) was a pittance compared with what Jesus went through for me. My offenses were actually a part of His sufferings, causing more agony for Him. Oh, to see the pain written on His face... I was humbled before Him, like a weaned child. (Psalms 131:2)

As I continue through the veil that same blood which announced me guilty then amazingly washes me clean (such a contradiction) which allows me to stand in the presence of God Almighty. As I pictured all this, continuing through the veil, I worshipped Him and then drifted off to a beautiful sleep.

The next morning before waking I had a dream where I saw before me what looked like a computer screen with dozens of photo icons on it. As I looked closer and zoomed in on one photo and then another, I saw they were all pictures of Ian. WOW! Up until that time I had not been able to picture Ian at all. Yet here before me was a whole screen full of pictures of Ian. 'Look into your face!' had been my protest but as I chose to look into my Lord's face and see the anguish due to my sin, He freed me from the poisoned arrows and ministered so preciously to me with that beautiful dream.

Chapter 39

I Used to Look Upon the Face of My Beloved Husband

I used to look upon the face of my beloved Ian. To face him as we engaged in conversation. Oh, how I would love to be able to look upon his face still now, to look into his eyes and he into mine. A look that goes far deeper, stretching back over years into lives lived and shared memories. That look as he would notice me as I walk into a room, his eyes dancing with that sparkle that I knew was only for me. 'Now, Oh Lord, instead You say to gaze upon Your face.'

'Seek the Lord, and his strength: seek his face evermore.' (Ps 105:4)
When thou saidst, seek ye my face; my heart said unto thee, Thy face, Lord, will I seek. (Ps 27:8)

It was getting late, but instead of going to bed I decided to look at the power–point of Ian again. As I watched the passing photos, each bringing with it a different memory, my eyes brimmed with tears. Those familiar feelings of grief, sorrow, and sadness were present with me again, like unwelcome guests who arrived unannounced and stayed too long.

There were photos of long ago and some more recent, some family shots, some of work, and some with grandchildren. In each photo I was looking for one person in particular; one face out of all the others – my beloved.

Whose face should I be seeking? Somewhere deep within came that question but to be honest, even though I long for the King of Kings and Lord of Lords, the great I AM, the creator and sustainer of life, part of me only wants to dwell on Ian.

'Sorry Lord, but as I sit here with sorrow as my acquaintance my reality is, I miss my husband, and it's him I want to see.'

Somehow, despite my disloyalty, the Lord reminds me of the fight, the battle not so long ago to look to Him, to His face and the miraculous outcome. *Yes, I remember well that amazing dream.* I look back at the computer screen. 'Now again Lord as I have been looking for Ian's face in all the photos You are saying, 'Julie, look into my face.' I stared blankly at the computer screen as I pondered these things.

The photo of Ian gazing at me on our wedding day staring at me gets my attention. *I love that photo.* However, now I want to look beyond my husband to my Lord. *How did I get here? I was bemoaning the fact that I couldn't see my husband and wished I could see him rather than to look upon God.* Still looking at the screen but not focusing properly it seems as though the eyes of the Lord are looking through the eyes of the photo, looking straight at me. I feel totally enveloped in His love, so cherished, so, so, who I am meant to be. I so totally do not deserve this. He is faithful when I am not.

'Lord, I know it was You who directed me to look through the power–point, to look for Ian's face in all those photos; to feel ever so deeply the pain of loss; to wish and desire so much that he was still with me ... all this, to show me that to the same degree and intensity I should desire You and Your presence, to look for Your face and into Your eyes.'

Chapter 40

My Whole Heart!

I wrote the following in 2013 before Ian went to be with the Lord:

Throughout the Psalms it speaks of seeking God with our whole heart. I have been so challenged by this – having to be honest with myself as to what has the attention of my heart, my mind, my thoughts.

When I sing, 'I Surrender All' do I really mean it, I mean really? or am I guilty with the Pharisees when Jesus stated, 'This people draweth nigh unto me with their mouth and honoureth me with their lips, but their heart is far from Me.' (Matt 15:8) The song continues, 'I will ever love and trust Him.' Oh, how fickle I am, saying I will ever trust Him when mostly I try and do things in my own strength and ability. When trouble strikes, I often give in to frustration, doubt, and defeat – hardly ever trusting.

Yet this is what is needed and should be normal in the Christian's life: total surrender and trust in our Saviour and Lord; being so totally awestruck by His majesty, love, and presence that we would continue to sing and live out the rest of the song 'in His presence daily live.'

'And thou shalt Love the Lord thy God with all thy heart, and with all thy soul, and with all they mind, and with all thy strength: this is the first commandment.' – Mark 23:30

It is now April 25th, 2014 and as I read that journal entry again, I cannot help thinking about the theme God seems to have for me at present. 'Father, You keep challenging me with the phrase, 'Julie, I want all of your heart.' Can't I keep just a little bit for Ian? It is so hard to say that You can have ALL my heart. Yet my thoughts go back to before Ian and I were married: when I was about sixteen, You asked me to choose between Ian and You. It was so hard back then but I knew I had to choose You and You gave Ian back to me anyway. I guess you are asking the same thing of me now but in a different context.'

'I well remember Your faithfulness in the first few weeks after Ian's passing into glory. As I fell on You, You caught me, ever so gently. You not only comforted me in such a real way, but You brought, with Your comforting arms around me, the knowledge that Ian was there in Spirit with me as well.'

'So, yes Lord, my whole heart. It belongs to You. I will seek after You and set my thoughts upon You.'

The Dream

A couple of mornings later, just before waking, I had a dream about Ian. This was amazing as until the photo icon dream with pictures of Ian, I had been unable to dream of him prior to this.

My dream unfolded with me sitting outside with Ian's mum. We were looking at a field. There was a fence before us, and Ian was in the field playing with some of the children. It was not unlike watching a movie on a screen played out in front of us as we commented on memories of Ian and the children.

It was a pleasant, joyful time. Then Ian came over to us as if coming out of the screenplay into our reality. He sat sort of on the fence which in fact was more like a stump. He held his hand out to me and I put my hand on his. To my surprise, I could actually feel his hand. And I mean feel! I was shocked because it was so real.

I looked at him, into his eyes, trying to comprehend. 'I can feel your hand, I can feel you!'

'So!' A smile grew on his face.

My mind was summersaulting. *Where am I? Where is Ian? What is happening here?* 'I can really feel you!'

His smile continued but this time with a glint and with that same gentle assuredness said, 'That's the way it is meant to be.'

Wow! We then embraced.

It felt so real that I immediately awoke. I shook my head in disbelief. *Did that really happen*? My mind was still summersaulting but oh what a 'wow.'

Praise God! I willingly gave Him all my heart, and He gave my husband back to me in an amazingly realistic dream. Our God is so awesome and so real. He knows where to meet us and what will bless us, much more than we know ourselves.

Chapter 41

Nowhere Else To Go

It was May 2nd, 2014. I knew winter had arrived as I felt the chill of the air and saw the starkness of the leafless tree out my window. Had this chill of winter also seeped within me or was there another reason for this gloom in my heart? I picked up the devotional book I have been reading lately and read the following by George Macdonald:

> 'How often do we look upon God as our last
> and feeble resource?
> We go to Him because we have nowhere else to go.
> And then we learn that the storms of life have drawn us
> Not upon the rocks, but into the desired haven.'

Nowhere else to go! Oh, how true this is of my situation now. The coldness and gloom resonate with these words as now, more than ever before, I have nowhere else to go; nowhere else to go since Ian is not here. That statement seems strange, weird, abnormal, as it has been Ian and Julie for such a long time. Now it is just ...Julie. That does not have a nice ring to it. It pains, it stings, it jars. Yet it is my reality, I cannot change it.

'Lord, I don't want to be just another widow, another statistic. I do not want to be put into a box labelled, 'Widow,' only to fulfil its prophecy and everyone's understanding of it. There must be a bigger reason Father, You must have a good reason for this, a good reason to take my husband.'

I remembered again the words in a song, 'death where is your sting, grave where is your victory?' These words originally come from the Bible, found in I Corinthians 15:5. To a Christian, death is not meant to have a sting or to have victory over them. However, today I do not feel too victorious.

I looked up another passage of scripture: *'Now if we be dead with Christ, we believe that we shall also live with him: Knowing that Christ being raised from the dead dieth no more; death hath no more dominion over him. For in that he died, he died unto sin once: but in that he liveth, he liveth unto God. Likewise reckon ye also yourselves to be dead indeed unto sin, but alive unto God through Jesus Christ our Lord.'* – Romans 6:8–11, 23 (emphasis added)

I have been here before. I need to not only see and believe these words of God but to live them; to reckon myself alive to God. I need to let the truth of God's Word chase away the chills of my heart and instead flood it with the truth, the life of Jesus.

Sometime later I was visiting Ian's gravesite. I sat down on the grass. Thoughts of Ian filled my mind. 'I miss you so much. It's so hard facing life without you.' I knew he was not there, but it gave me the opportunity to let my feelings have words. I thought of his lifeless body in that wooden tomb underneath the sod. *What body?* I did not want to think about it. Tears quietly formed and rolled down my cheeks.

I found myself asking those same questions I had previously. 'Lord, I don't want to be just another widow. You must have a good reason for this.' Owning up to something and putting voice to it really helps for as I said it, a firm trust reaching back to so many of God's faithfulness' came upon me. His Spirit was moving upon me. Reassuring me, He did have a good reason!

I was surprised how quickly an hour passed. However, I come away with a sense of peace that God does all things well, and the bigger reason will slowly unfold. He meets us where we are as we wait upon Him. He met me and gently answered with calm reassurance, 'I AM in control.'

'Trust in the LORD with all thine heart; and lean not unto thine own understanding. In all thy ways acknowledge him, and he shall direct thy paths.' Proverbs 3:5,6

Chapter 42

Your Way O Lord is in the Sanctuary
– My Time Warp

The setting: July 10th, 2014 out west, near Narrandera, where each year we have a three week lamb–marking job on a large sheep property. This job is the only one where the younger children and I also go along to be a part of the team. I am the cook for the team. However, today I joined the crew heading out to the sheep as two of the team members were feeling unwell. While out working I realised the only times I had put in a day's work in the paddock, lamb marking or pushing up sheep for pregnancy scanning, had been with Ian as the team leader.

Of course, this time Ian was not there. I notice my son, David, the team leader, doing and saying things much as Ian would have. During the times of waiting for the next lamb moments of contemplation came.

Had David always led the team this way or is it that I, so missing Ian, so wishing he were here, see him at every turn?

And is that Ian's jacket David is wearing? Probably not but I'm sure Ian wore one very similar.

Everyone around me continues working unaware of the emotions trying to lay hold on me. It is hard to grasp the stark reality of it all! I notice lambs are waiting in the cradles and I breathe a heavy sigh as I step forward to continue treating the marked lambs.

Today, July 16th, I had to drive to the office on the property to send a fax. As I drive out the gate on the return journey, I notice the sheep yards to my left. I slow down before pulling to a stop. Thoughts came flooding into my mind. *Just a year ago I was here; Ian was he*re.

On that day, a year previous, Ian had suggested I bring lunch out instead of packing it in the morning, as he was working close at the homestead yards. It also meant the younger boys could come, which they loved. I brought out some hot soup which was such a blessing as there was a cold wind blowing. We sat in the shed to shelter from the wind and enjoyed the simple but hot meal.

The meal finished, we returned to work. Shortly into the work, Ian smiled and pointed behind us to a small set of yards. 'Look at Shiloh and the manager's son. Look how they are handling those lambs all by themselves.' Shiloh was just six years old and his offsider, only four. They were in the yards behind us doing their own sheep work, drafting lambs with horns from those without horns and doing an amazing job.

As these memories of a year previous came vividly back to me, so too did the emotions of grief and sorrow, those ever-present but most unwelcome friends.

Oh God, I miss him! I miss him so much! How I wish it weren't so! I struggled, not wanting to accept the reality of my life now but wanting rather to return to a year gone past. *Can't we just rewind? Can I somehow stay here in this time zone of last year? Can it be frozen, bottled, preserved with me wrapped up in it?* I was stuck. I could proceed no further and yet life was calling me on.

As I struggled with these feelings, the words from the morning's Psalm came back to me, 'Thy way O God is in the sanctuary!' (Psalm 77:13) My answer, my way out of the engulfing emotions I was experiencing, was in the sanctuary. So, there I went and there in God's presence is my husband, Ian, totally immersed in the wonder, the beauty, and the love of God. This is where Ian is, not back there a year ago. He is home. What a place! This is home where I am headed and where I want to be, not stuck in some time warp of the past.

In reflecting on this, God gave me my answer: If I were there where Ian is, there is no way I would want to come back here. So too, for Ian, how can I wish him to be back here after experiencing the full and perfect reality of God and all He has for us?

Praise God! I was back in the place and time God has for me. I was then able to continue the drive back to the shearer's quarters with a fresh understanding of our awesome God, the reality of His presence now and the amazing inheritance He has for me.

Chapter 43

Looking unto Jesus

It is July 31st, nearly eight months without Ian. I constantly am having to look to the Lord, at what He has done for me, to delight in Him and His ways to cope with the everyday reality of not having my husband. This week for me has been hard and depressing after being away for three weeks working with the family business and now having to face the enormity of all there is to do. There is the end of financial year work for the business and myself, decisions with the farm, housework, a garden to tend, schooling with the children, and my mum to visit in the nursing home.

Also, I have had three South Africans living and working with us for a couple of months. We have a small house, and from last Friday till Sunday my son and daughter in law with their four children were here as well, 19 people in all staying in my not so big house. Everything was becoming all too much for me. It was crowding in on me.

There had been a spark of hope in all this with the possibility of someone coming to help with the farm work. I had started to feel some of the pressure lifting from me. However, the possibility dissipated and came to nothing, making the enormity of the task before me pressing down harder than before.

I had retreated to my room to try and escape the suffocating feeling, to be alone with my emotions apart from the throng of people in my space. I did not want to be around anyone. I cried out to God. I fell before Him, seeking His way, and His answer.

Praise God! He met me and showed me again what He has done for me, giving me the strength at that moment to face the immediate, just to make it to the dinner table to eat with the family.

I know that He will show me and guide me through all the things which have been crowding in upon me, just one step at a time. This evening it was just to make it to the dinner table. It's Him and me now, and with Him, I can do all things. He will show me, strengthen me, and provide me with the people or things I need to manage all these areas in my life for He promises to be my provider. When I am weak, then I am strong, because He can be strong in me.

Looking unto Jesus!!

Chapter 44

The Pineapple

As I was going through a drawer in my bedroom, I came across a pineapple cut-out with words written on it. I had cut it out quite some time ago after listening to the Pineapple story on CD told by Arthur Koning. Arthur's testimony convicted me concerning giving up rights which I felt I deserved. I decided to make a reminder and so cut out the pineapple and wrote on it the following:

I give up my Right to Have a Husband Who:
- is home most days and nights, i.e., not working away from home
- is actively involved in home-schooling
- instigates and leads family devotions and worship
- has time to keep the shed and yard tidy
- is here more to discipline the children
- doesn't get tired or grumpy

Oh, Lord! All those so-called rights I thought were mine. I would so love to have my husband still here with me, and would it matter if he was not here most nights? Would it matter that he did not take a more active part in the schooling of the children? So what! Would I be upset if he did not lead family worship how I thought he should or if he didn't get the yard and shed tidied? Would I still complain, even if only in my thoughts, about his workload and being away so much? Would I be upset if he was tired at times and seemingly hard on the children?

On the other hand, would I praise God that at least I did have a husband, a husband who loved me, who loved our children and who loved God?

Oh, Lord, the emotion runs thick, trying to engulf me, trying to drown me under a sea of 'what if's' and 'if only's'. I would hope to do things differently now if I could have the chance again. I chide myself: a*nother chance? Too late! You missed your chance.*

It pains me so much now when I hear of people so easily throwing their marriages away. Oh Lord, it means little to them and yet so much to me.

The image of Christ and the church, His bride, is a wonderful mystery, the husband/wife relationship being a picture of that mystery. The Lord has been unravelling this mystery more to me. Now with this increased understanding of the importance of marriage, I have no husband to play out this mystery of glorifying God through the relationship. I can only encourage other wives to do so. What is your view of God and His bride? How is the image of your relationship with God as part of the bride of Christ playing out in your marriage?

'Father God, I pray you would strengthen Christian marriages. That husbands and wives would display within their relationship with one another, the beautiful mystery of that union between You and Your most beloved bride.'

Chapter 45

Treasure Untold

All is quiet as the children are in bed. This gives me time to sit at my computer. I stare at the background picture, a photo from our wedding day. In it I am about to enter the bridal car while Ian looks on. WOW – That look! They say a picture can say a thousand words. Ian is totally besotted, filled with joy, full of love and desire. He has eyes only for his new bride. He is totally unaware and disinterested in the crowd around him. I see him thinking, 'Wow! She's mine.'

I love that photo! What a 'hunk' of a man. No wonder I fell in love with him. But ... he is gone. Every part of my being feels the starkness of those words as they sweep over and right through me, engulfing me.

Oh God! I miss him!

It is October 20th, over ten months since Ian drove off to work on that fateful day, the last time I saw him and felt that last kiss. As I looked at that photo again, I saw those expressive, longing, enraptured eyes. How I want that now. I sense the Lord speaking ever so gently to me, 'All the love you have ever felt from Ian was only a small measure of the love I have for you. Any time you felt loved by Ian, it was, in fact, me loving you through him.'

The words bring a deeper understanding. As I continue looking at the picture of Ian, I begin to see in those eyes, the longing desire and rapture the Lord has for me. How unexplainably precious that is. I want to savour that, to wrap it up and hold it forever. I look at more photos of Ian and myself, but my eyes are only upon Ian, especially his eyes. The photo on my computer background suddenly comes up, and I pause. My thoughts turn to my Lord and what He said to me.

That pause and stillness bring forth the verse, 'Be still and know that I am God.' (Ps 46:10) In the pause, in the stillness, in the pondering on God, He again spoke to me in that still small voice, 'Julie, I have treasures untold for you.' WOW!!

Chapter 46
I Can't Do This

It is early November and my week thus far has been one of trying to get business matters finished and out of the way. I have also been continuing to sort out one of the bedrooms, now running into the third week of doing so due to numerous interruptions including the business work. However, first up this morning I needed to check on the chickens and garden as there had been a bit of neglect earlier in the week.

As I walked out the door, I noticed the blueberry pot–plant my son and daughter in law had given me. It did not look vibrant and healthy as in previous days. A closer look revealed that only half the dirt remained in the pot. Obviously, the pot had been knocked over by boy or ball or both, spilling out half the contents. This was not the first time it had happened, but the contents had not spilled out like this before.

It is amazing how one's emotions can change so swiftly. Chickens and garden now forgotten as steady calmness gave way to heated anger and frustration. Somewhere from within came the heat and steam as of a simmering volcano. *Who did this? When did this happen? Why couldn't they have put the dirt back in and watered it?* I picked up the spilled dirt, trying to restore the pot to how it was.

Really, it was not such a big deal. It was only a pot plant. I was able to add more dirt and water it BUT ...

... with this frustration on top of others from the previous weeks, I suddenly saw before me all that needed doing: a house to organise, a garden to weed, an orchard to establish, a farm to run, cows to feed, fences to fix, a shed to build, chicken pens to complete, a business to run, and children to train and teach. So why would I be so upset about a knocked over pot plant? It was much more than a pot plant – it was the last straw.

Feelings of despair and hopelessness came flooding over me. 'GOD, I CAN'T DO THIS!!' I shouted it out loud.

As I stood there helplessly in my desperation the Lord reminded me of the wonderful words I had read that morning and shared with the children:

Psalm 26 – 'Judge me, O LORD; for I have walked in mine integrity! I have trusted also in the LORD; therefore I shall not slide. Examine me, O LORD, and prove me; try my reins and my heart. For thy lovingkindness is before mine eyes: and I have walked in thy truth.... I will wash mine hands in innocency: so will I compass thine altar, O LORD: That I may publish with the voice of thanksgiving, and tell of all thy wondrous works. LORD, I have loved the habitation of thy house, and the place where thine honour dwelleth ... My foot standeth in an even place: in the congregations will I bless the LORD.'

Judge me, O LORD; for I have walked in mine integrity! I have trusted also in the LORD! *Walked in integrity? Trusted in the Lord?* 'For thy lovingkindness is before mine eyes and I have walked in thy truth.' *Was His loving kindness before my eyes? Was I walking in His truth?*

One thing for sure I was being tried. In the book of James it says to be doers of the Word, not just hearers. Jesus likens the person who only hears his words to those who build their house on the sand which, when the wind and floods come, collapses. Those who hear and obey are like a building on the rock which outlasts the storm, standing firm.

Here I have a choice: sand or rock; a house that stands the test or one that falls; only hear or hear and actively do; walk in His truth.

I choose to hear, believe, and do what the Word of God says. 'Forgive me Lord for not trusting, for giving way to feelings other than thanksgiving. I will choose to listen and obey. Redeem me and be merciful unto me. My foot stands in an even place now so that I can say, 'I shall not slide, and as for me I will walk in my integrity. Thank you, Lord. You have again changed me.'

I returned inside and sat down at my desk and before long I had ideas coming to help direct a couple of the children. My mind was clear to work through and implement these ideas. Praise God!

Chapter 47
Lead Me to the Rock That is Higher Than I

Earlier today I asked the children to do a chore. When I finally checked on them instead of doing the task given, some were playing with toys and others were reading. My chest heaves up and down as a sigh escapes from my lips. *Yet again!* This was happening because I had not been hovering over the children, making sure things were being done, and so they went AWOL. In a week's time it will be 12 months since Ian's passing. Can I use that as an excuse?

We read Psalm 11 this morning: 'In the Lord put I my trust; how say ye to my soul, Flee as a bird to your mountain? For, lo, the wicked bend their bow, they make ready their arrow upon the string, that they may privily shoot at the upright in heart. If the foundations be destroyed, what can the righteous do? The Lord is in His holy temple, the Lord's throne is in heaven; His eyes behold, His eyelids try the children of men. The Lord trieth the righteous …'

Well, I had some arrows flying. Lies from the enemy: 'What's the point of spending time in the Word each morning with the children if they don't learn anything? What is the point if they can't follow commands? Haven't I been here before?

How long do I have to put up with this? I cannot train my children properly.'

GOD HELP ME!!!

As I entered the laundry, more thoughts assailed me, arrows striking, penetrating, wounding. 'I'm not a good mother. I cannot train my children properly. Without Ian here it is hopeless!' Painful emotion overcame me. I picked up a basket of washing and proceeded to hang it up. As the clothes were hung tears trickled down my face. There was no doubt that I was being tried. I needed to climb my mountain. Washing hung; I began the trek: out the gate, through one fence, under another, past the dam and up the hill.

Lead me to the rock that is higher than I. These words came to mind but so did other thoughts. On Sunday someone remarked about one of my boys, stating that he would be every mother's dream for their son.

Ha, what about these boys? Every mother's dream? I feel so inadequate!

'Lead me to the rock that is higher than I.' I repeated it for I knew that there would be my answer. Out of breath, I reached the top and slumped down on the ground against the large rock. The sun streamed down upon me. I had to shield my face.

'God, I'm not leaving here till you change me. I'm not going back no matter how long I have to stay here.' I was desperate and resolute. It was not so much the house, the children, or even the situation. I did not want to return to those feelings and emotions, the lies trying to dictate my life.

I pressed my back against the hard surface of the rock feeling its solidness, something I could lean on. It was not going to move, not going anywhere. Yes, the psalmist speaks of God being the rock. *Lead me to the rock that is higher than I.* I focused on those words, their meaning, and the one who is that rock.

'Yes, Julie, I am that rock, I do not move, I do not change. You can lean on me wherever you are for I am with you always.'

A word directly from the Lord can be so full of meaning and understanding and can so quickly change everything. 'Oh, Lord. You were right there with me when I saw the pot plant, with me and the AWOL children, but I didn't lean on You. You teach me so many things. And, of course, I already knew You are the rock I can lean on, yet I did not lean. I said that I would build upon the rock and not the sand, to hear and obey, to put it into action, rather than hear and forget. Forgive my lack of trust,'

My focus had changed, and things became clearer. *The Lord is in His holy temple. I need to pass through the veil torn for me into His presence, sprinkled clean by the blood of Jesus.*

As I did, I sensed not only the presence of the Lord but also my husband, Ian. I felt as if we were sitting together, both leaning on the rock, side by side in the presence of the Lord.

As I pondered earlier events and now my husband beside me, I also thought of times as his wife I had not leaned on the Lord. In my mind, I said to Ian, 'Please forgive me for my complaining, for getting upset and cross, for not being as good a wife as you deserved.'

It seemed as if he were before me, looking straight at me. 'There's nothing to forgive. You are more beautiful than ever.'

Wow! What wife doesn't want to hear that from her husband, especially when years have passed and wrinkles appear and things generally begin to sag?

'For thou hast made him most blessed for ever: thou hast made him exceeding glad with thy countenance' (Psalm 21:6). God's countenance, His face was beholding, looking, smiling at me, as was Ian. It was as if Ian and the Lord were bonded into one and the Lord Himself was also saying those words to me. How amazingly wonderful and affirming!

Praise be to God. As I walked down from my mountain, I sang, 'You are my strength when I am weak. You are the treasure that I seek. You are my all in all. ...Worthy is Your name.' – Dennis Jernigan

Chapter 48

With Christ in My Vessel

With Christ in My Vessel I Can Smile at the Storm' is part of the song Jesus reminded me of this morning as I read the following from my devotional:

'Can strength be born out of weakness; Courage out of fear; Joy out of sorrow; confidence out of feelings of inadequacy; Compassion out of pain; New life out of loss? When we stand in the middle of a life−storm, it seems as if the storm has become our way of life. We cannot see a way out. We are unable to chart a course back to smoother waters. We feel defeated and broken. Will that brokenness produce a cynicism that will keep us forever in the mire of 'if only' thinking? Or will we yield up that brokenness to the resources of One who calms the wind and the waves, heals the broken hearted, and forgives the most grievous of sins? The choice is ours.' – Verdell Davis

I sang the song, and the story found in Matthew 8:26 came to mind. Jesus rebuked the disciples for having such little faith in the face of a huge and terrifying storm. The disciples were seasoned fishermen, this was their life. They knew these waters, and they knew about storms, and this one was no small storm, it was the storm of all storms. They honestly thought they would all drown. So why does Jesus say they have little faith?

According to Jesus, there was nothing to fear. Yet in the disciples' minds there was every reason to fear regarding this circumstance. If you know this story, then you know that in the end they had nothing to fear. However, these fishermen were right in the middle of the storm and could not see the end, only their fears in the moment causing them to believe a false end. They only knew what they were experiencing.

Then Jesus rebuked the storm, everything became calm, and they reached the shore. Jesus' words to them earlier were to get into the boat and go to the other side. There was no storm at the time, all was calm. Jesus never said anything about drowning in the middle of the lake. Jesus expected them to reach the other side safely.

Jesus knew the disciples would reach the shore alive. I am to have total faith in His words, that they are true and will come to pass. God knows the beginning and end of all things including each of the circumstances of my life. I have faced many storms over this past year, and Jesus has calmed every one of them so I can trust him with the storms that will no doubt continue to arise in my life.

'Jesus, just like the disciples, You want me to know the truth of who You are and the power of Your words in my life, to make me victorious in all things. I pray that I will not give into fear, that I will trust You in the storms, knowing I will arrive on the other side safely.'

'No weapon that is formed against thee shall prosper and every tongue that shall rise against thee in judgement, thou shalt condemn. This is the heritage of the servants of the Lord.'
– Isaiah 54:17

Chapter 49

A Heavenly Perspective

F ollowing is a description of what happened the day Ian left us: David had been working with his dad, Ian, drafting sheep on a hot and dusty December day. Ian was standing drafting ewes while David was pushing the sheep into the drafting race. David looked up noticing one sheep had gone the wrong way and then another. He yelled out to his dad to let him know but noticed he was not responding but standing motionless, holding the drafting gate. As time slowed down, he watched his father release his grip on the gate, bend at the knees and fall backwards with a thump to the ground.

David leapt over a fence, shutting a gate on the rest of the sheep, in an effort to reach his dad, still yelling out to him. His first thought was he had fainted in the heat and perhaps had hit his head on falling. He dialled 000 and with guidance started resuscitation which he continued until the ambulances arrived, some 30 minutes or later.

This was all to no avail as God had called Ian home and no one was going to bring him back. He had fought a good fight, run a good race; the fight and the race were over: it was time for the prize.

It is hard to think of your dad being home at last, heavenward and receiving a prize in the aftermath of trying to save him from dying. Slathered in sweat from the ordeal in stifling heat, wishing, hoping for signs of reviving, signs of life, David cried out to his father, 'Dad, please don't go, Dad, please don't go!' He was beside himself with utter grief and helplessness.

After the ambulances had arrived and after continuing efforts to revive Ian, they informed David that he had gone. David then had the task of informing me. In emotional and faltering words, he tried to explain what had just happened: 'Dad . . . has gone to be with . . . Jesus.'

However, within a couple of minutes of the pronouncement from the attending paramedic that Ian had gone, David looked up to see a huge branch of a nearby tree come crashing to the ground. Later in retelling this event, David approached it from a heavenly perspective stating that the angel who came to get Dad must have had L–plates on his chariot and as he took off and, not see the tree, caught the side of it causing the branch to fall.

Then again, eleven days later, the day after the graveside funeral and thanksgiving service, just after lunch, I walked outside to check the washing only to see one half of a tree slowly fall thunderously to the ground, just scraping the side of the shed with the topmost branches.

Reporting this astonishing event to those inside, someone commented, 'Dad must have arrived with the same L–plate angel driving the chariot as the day he left. He must have come to see all the ceremonies yesterday and now today as he was taking off hit not just a branch, but half a tree.' This brought laughter from us all.

I tend to think Ian might have been the one to blame not an L–plate angel as I can just see him jumping at the chance to have a go at driving this new form of transportation. (After all, he did get his semi–trailer licence last year but never had a chance to use it.)

Having a heavenly perspective helps you to see things quite differently, and in this case, quite amusingly.

'Let not your heart be troubled: ye believe in God, believe also in me. In my Father's house are many mansions: if it were not so, I would have told you. I go to prepare a place for you. And if I go and prepare a place for you, I will come again, and receive you unto myself; that where I am, there ye may be also.' John 14:1–3

Chapter 50

Life Abundantly

One really is at a loss knowing what to say to someone who loses his or her spouse, especially suddenly. I have been that person and had a fragment of an idea, a fear, a horror of such a thing happening but could not imagine what it must be like in reality. Now I have been on the other side of that, living that reality, and with losing my husband suddenly, other things pale in comparison. I feel for the person trying to know what to say to me and understand their awkwardness.

This is without a doubt, the most significant trial in my whole life, and yet God has given me so much grace to enable me to know the victory and overcoming power which belongs to every Christian, all the time, no matter what they face – if only we would truly believe! If only we would take God at His word and believe it. When God said, 'Let there be light,' there was light. If God says He has borne our griefs and carried our sorrows, then He has. Since Jesus has already carried our grief and sorrow, why would we want to try and carry them ourselves?

As I face life without my husband questions often repeatedly come to mind. Frequently with tears and laments, I present them to the Lord: 'God why, how come? What am I meant to do? I cannot cope! This is all too much! Help! God, I miss him!'

As I quiet myself before Him and pause from my ranting, He answers me and fills me with joy, not of this world. People are astounded when they see me and hear what God is doing for and in me. I find myself ministering to others instead of them ministering to me. In awkwardness they approach me, not knowing how to offer condolences and instead I am telling them what God just did for me last week, yesterday, or that morning. I am seeing more and more that this is the normal Christian walk, exactly what Jesus and Paul said:

'I am come that they might have life, and that they might have it more abundantly.' John 10:10

'He that believeth on me, as the scriptures hath said, out of his belly shall flow rivers of living water.' John 7:38

'Now unto him that is able to do exceeding abundantly above all that we ask or think, according to the power that worketh in us...' Eph 3:20

Do these scriptures say we can have life more abundant, and living water flowing in and through us to others only when things are going well; only when life is wonderful and things are sailing smoothly along? Having so-called abundant life only when the sun shines down on us does not show as much power or victory as when the days are dark. That is when we appreciate the light shining through, and that's when others see it more clearly.

A question put to me at one time challenged me big time: 'Do you really believe that the Bible is the Word of God?' My reply was 'yes, of course' and then, 'If so, why aren't you living like you believe it? 'Ouch! Those words were like an arrow penetrating right through to my heart. *Yes, why aren't I living like that?* That question has often hounded me over the years, causing me to ponder, *where is the abundant life promised?*

Since then, as I have taken those words on board, I have read the Bible differently. I have been asking God to make His Word real to me. Therefore, when He says we have risen with Him, I believe it. When He says to put on the garment of praise for the spirit of heaviness, I believe it. When He says we are daily loaded with benefits, I believe it. And when He says He has borne all my griefs and sorrows, I believe that too.

That sounds amazing but in reality, I still struggle with all those things: seeing everything as benefits, praising Him when I'm feeling down, and believing He has taken my grief and sorrow. These do not flow easily, and I often argue with God about these things in His word as they are not usually my experience or feelings but rather the opposite.

In the end, however, when I submit to the truth of His Word rather than my fickle feelings, He wins out. With that, He brings me deliverance and makes me alive to those truths, filling me with that living water and more abundant life.

Even though my husband is gone from this earth and my life has changed drastically forever, I have joy and peace beyond understanding. My Lord Jesus has the answers to all my doubts, my questions, my lack of trust. I cannot praise Him enough.

BELOVED

I have no down to earth practical answers other than what I have shared, but it has been the answer to all my down to earth problems. He has answered them all. May He do the same for you!

'Death is swallowed up in victory. O death, where is thy sting? O grave, where is thy victory? The sting of death is sin and the strength of sin is the law. But thanks be to God, which giveth us the victory through our Lord Jesus Christ.'
I Corinthians 15:54–57

Chapter 51

The Faith of a Child

Today is December 9th, 2014, exactly 12 months, one year since Ian went to be with the Lord. I had amazingly finished the first draft of this book and wanted to present it to the children this morning. The first writing of this book came together from start to finish in less than a month which was totally the work of God.

Our family Bible reading for today was Psalms 41–45. In presenting this book to them it seemed fitting to read chapter 22, 'Blessed is He That Considers the Poor.' It is what the Lord had shown me back in January concerning Psalm 41. The theme of the chapter is 'What is Life?'

I asked the children, 'Is there anything special you would like to do today in celebration of dad?'

Jaden was the first to speak. 'Can we go to the grave-site today?'

One of the other children screwed up their nose in response. 'Why would you want to do that? Dad isn't there anymore.'

A discussion then started about people who did not believe the truth of the Bible and who think the grave is the end of it all.

Jaden, ten years old at the time, said, 'How could anyone believe that? I couldn't ever imagine that. I know where Dad is and that's not in the grave!'

Praise God! How many ten–year–old boys who have lost their father say words like those, with complete conviction and without being angry that their Dad was taken from them? 'Praise You Lord!'

A true heavenly perspective!

Chapter 52

Firsts

Lots can happen in four months, six months, twelve months. For me, the biggest, most life-changing, of course, was Ian's sudden and totally unexpected death on December 9th, 2013. Grief counselling includes the importance of being aware of the impact of first-time events since the passing of a loved one can have on you. Things like birthdays and anniversaries can be a trigger for emotions of grief and sorrow to burst upon one's life. Below is the series of such events since the departing of Ian:

In Four Months
- Ian's body sent to Sydney for an autopsy as the local person was away, thus waiting for the release of the body made the funeral and thanksgiving service eleven days after Ian's passing.
- Dec 14th – employee, Matt's wedding. Two of our sons were groomsmen. We all attended.
- Our bore broke down.

- Dec 20th – Ian's graveside funeral for the family at Coolac. Thanksgiving service in Yass.
- Dec 21st – rainwater tanks ran dry.
- Jan – I wrote an apology letter to Ian's family.
- Jan 31st – A good friend's husband went to be with the Lord after a long battle with cancer.
- Feb 9th – Baptisms of our three youngest boys.
- Feb 16th – Ian's birthday.
- Death certificate took weeks to come, finally arrived but arrived without a cause of death.
- Feb –Ian's youngest sister's, 40th birthday party – First time seeing all Ian's family since the funeral. Ten hours travel, we all attended.
- Mar –Ian's oldest sister and brother in law's 40th anniversary. Ten hours travel, I attended alone.
- Mar 14th – Birth of granddaughter, (grandchild no. 9).
- April – Attended nephew's wedding in Melbourne.
- April 14th – 35th wedding anniversary.
- Easter – Immediate family all get–together
- April – Still no cause of death.
- April –A French guy comes to stay and work with us.

In Six Months
- May – another French guy came to stay and work for us.
- Three boys start playing AFL football.
- Business problems – vehicles, computers, clients, employees.
- May 20th – Birth of grandson, (grandchild no. 10).
- June – Aug – four South Africans stayed and worked for us.

- June 21st – ATI home–school regional conference – where I shared a testimony.
- June 30th – end of financial year.

Up to Twelve Months
- August 24th – Another big 'first' was son, Raphael's eighteenth birthday party.
- Sep 19th – I shared a short testimony at a mother's retreat.
- Oct 5th – Son, David's 30th birthday party. I helped Beck to organise the party at my home.
- Oct 23rd – My birthday.
- Dec 9th – Anniversary of Ian going to be with the Lord.
- Dec – Children playing instruments at the yearly Kaniva Senior Citizens concert. Ian had been there last year just three days before his death.

Mixed in all that were lots of birthdays, lots of memories, lots of sorrows and lots of God's presence.

Chapter 53

A Mighty Woman of God

God brought someone into my life in April 2013, and an instant friendship was formed, an unusual friendship: a seventy–year–old widow who lives on her own, married twice but who never bore any children. In contrast, I was 52, had eleven children, eight still at home, three married and eight grandchildren.

Little did I realise the impact this lady would have upon my life. Neither of us knew what lay ahead – that I too would be a widow less than eight months from our initial introduction. Shona only met Ian once and saw in him a mighty man of God, something which he questioned. I am so glad she got to meet him that one time.

After she received the news about Ian's sudden passing, Shona organised to come and stay with us in the week leading up to the funeral. She helped take charge of the children and the running of the house, something I appreciated so much. But she also understood what I was going through as she had walked that dark vale herself.

God carried me so much in those first weeks and months, and I would often share with others that I felt like part of me was standing looking on at myself in amazement at what God was doing, even using me to minister to others.

We had extra family staying in those initial days, so Shona shared my bed with me, and we would have deep sharing times. As she discovered more about my family and me, about some of the things we have been through and the rawness of the present trial she said to me, 'You mighty woman of God!'

My response was, 'Thank you, Lord!' And then, I burst out laughing with Shona doing likewise.

We laughed and laughed, uncontrollably. I was trying to tell Shona why I was laughing but could not get the words out due to the laughter that kept tumbling out of my mouth every time I tried to speak. Finally, between my laughing fits, I was able to get out the reason for my jollity. I told her that it was because I had responded to her initial statement with 'Thankyou Lord' rather than anything else and because that it is exactly what I want to be – a mighty woman of God.

I knew it wasn't anything to do with me; it was all God's doing and with that realisation I said to Shona, 'I feel as if self, flesh, is falling from me. This is a most wonderful place to be and who could possibly imagine or understand that I could be laughing like this when my husband died just a week ago.' We both laughed again.

There was a faint knock on the door, and it opened slightly. My daughter, Michaela put her head in, confusion written all over her face, 'Are you OK?' Upon seeing the smiles on our faces and with her face just as confused, she backed out and closed the door. We continued laughing and sharing the goodness of God.

Since then, I have read that one of the therapies suggested for grief is laugh therapy. Well, God knew that before any psychologist ('A merry heart doeth good like a medicine, but a broken spirit drieth the bones'–Prov 17:22). God had his own laugh therapy organised for me.

How does one become a mighty woman of God? Through being brought low, through being stripped of self and desiring God more than all others; by being willing to trust no matter what; to be able to say and live out that God does all things well. Of myself, I am full of pride and all things contrary to God, but with and through Jesus I no longer live, but He lives in me. As I take Him at His word, I can say, 'I can do all things through Christ who strengthens me. I am weak, but He is strong. I am nothing but He is all, and He makes me a mighty woman of God!'

All Praise to His name!!

My Darling Wife
November 6th, 2013

My Darling Wife,
Julie
How I love you. You are my friend & lover,
my companion, and helper.
You give good, sound advice so often.
You're amazing.

Thank you for all that you do for me.
I'm sorry that I don't acknowledge all of those things as I should –
Please forgive me.

I pray that I will encourage you and thank you more and more.
You are wonderful.

I really appreciate your encouragement
for all of us to walk closer in the Lord.
Lots of love, affection, and joy,

IAN

Epilogue

Twelve months have gone since Ian departed. Can I believe it? So much has transpired over those twelve months. It seems like only yesterday but also like a dream of long ago. I ponder this day a year ago: the phone call, the shock, the knot in my stomach, telling the children, having to ring family, facing a different future, – I lived through that?

Ian's life is a tale that will continue to be told in the lives of his children. He left them a wonderful heritage – one founded on and in the Word of God. Ian had a real and living relationship with God, and he is reaping the benefits of that, being continually in the presence of his Lord and Saviour, living in a paradise unimaginable. Our children are also reaping the benefits of that as they continue in their own relationship with God.

Part of the message given at Ian's memorial service was from John 12:24 'Except a corn of wheat fall into the ground and die, it abideth alone; but if it die, it bringeth forth much fruit.' We are to die to our self–life for God to produce much good fruit in us. Likewise, Ian's death is not for naught. The life he lived is not wasted but will go on to produce much good fruit in the lives of, not only his children, but many other people.

I lost my husband, my most dearly beloved, but I have gained so much. I can appreciate what others have been through and may be facing so much more keenly, especially those who grieve; my own relationship with God has deepened; I have come to know Him in a much more intimate way, and this book would not have been written if Ian were still here. I still miss him so, so much but the Lord makes up for it and has 'treasures untold for me.'

'My beloved is mine and I am His, and His banner over me is love.'

Acknowledgements

I want to acknowledge the real author – God Himself. This is really His story of His working in the life of an ordinary person, a hurting person, willing to trust Him and His Word. I also wish to thank Jenny Glazebrook especially for encouraging me in this endeavour and for the time she put in proofreading this book initially and prior to editing. To my wonderful family who have encouraged and supported me so much and for all those over the years who encouraged me to write a book.

D.O.L.L.

Daughters of Love & Light is a ministry hub for women and an independent publisher of Christian women's literature.

We believe in Christ-centred community, creativity, and calling.

Join the community
www.daughtersofloveandlight.com

www.ingramcontent.com/pod-product-compliance
Lightning Source LLC
Chambersburg PA
CBHW051434290426
44109CB00016B/1556